P9-CLO-845

The Employee Experience

The Employee Experience

How to Attract Talent, Retain Top Performers, and Drive Results

Tracy Maylett, EdD, and
Matthew Wride, JD

Cover design: Wiley

Published by John Wiley & Sons, Inc., Hoboken, New Jersey

Published simultaneously in Canada

For general information about our other products and services, please contact our Customer Care Department within the United States at (800) 762-2974, outside the United States at (317) 572-3993 or fax (317) 572-4002.

Wiley publishes in a variety of print and electronic formats and by print-on-demand. Some material included with standard print versions of this book may not be included in e-books or in print-on-demand. If this book refers to media such as a CD or DVD that is not included in the version you purchased, you may download this material at http://booksupport.wiley.com. For more information about Wiley products, visit www.wiley.com.

ISBN 978-1-119-29418-4 (cloth)
ISBN 978-1-119-29419-1 (ePDF)
ISBN 978-1-119-29420-7 (ePub)

Printed in the United States of America

10 9 8 7 6 5 4 3 2

Contents

To our families, our valued partners, friends, and the DecisionWise team—you make our Experience *magic*.

Foreword

When you ask employees how they approach their jobs, just over half of them say that they put in the least amount of work possible without getting fired. If this statistic is true, odds are the guy who recently assembled your grandfather's pacemaker didn't really care. One can only hope that surly pacemaker guy is actually part of the other half who are engaged in their work.

Until you understand who is putting in a full and smart effort each day—from producing pacemakers to driving Disney's Jungle Boat (you try telling the same dumb jokes twenty times a day)—you don't know where to focus your leadership attention. Who is fully engaged, but not in serving their customers—instead, they're engaged in serving themselves? Consider the artists who design shampoo and conditioner labels. They work hard to produce a product that will win all kinds of art awards. Of course, that means they use small, grey fonts (they're considered artsy and all the rage). Now, nobody over fifty who has the temerity to remove their glasses before entering the shower, can see the labels. Oh well, it's just shampoo and conditioner. But what if the stakes were higher?

As you look behind the engagement headlines, you're compelled to ask why so many people care so little about their work—or their customers. But you already know the answer, don't you? It's those darn Gen-Xers, Millennials, and other narcissists who are taking celebratory photos of themselves every time they chug a large soft drink or stand in front of a waterfall. When will people like that ever think about serving customers?

Perhaps we should look at this through a different lens. Maybe it's not because of their age, and they weren't simply born under the wrong star. It's not because they're selfish and lazy. There are dozens of factors that turn a job into, well, a job—and not a dream. If researchers could find those forces, and learn how to change them, leaders could move from complaining about low engagement to measuring and changing the experience. And, with a rise in employee engagement, so rises the customer experience.

That's just what Tracy Maylett and Matthew Wride did. They plowed through tens of thousands of cases and millions of data points, figured out what actually tips the scale of engagement, and are now sharing what you can do to attract and retain top performing employees by building the right employee experience for your organization.

Good for them. For me, I'm taking away two things from this. First, based upon the marvelous research and catchy writing they displayed, Maylett and Wride were fully engaged in writing this book. It's truly a work of passion. Second, I'm hoping that, when the day arrives, they can tell me the name of a fully engaged person who should build my pacemaker.

—Kerry Patterson
Coauthor of the *New York Times* bestseller
Crucial Conversations: Tools for Talking When Stakes Are High
January 2017

Introduction

> Engagement is a fundamental human need. It is a power that resides in most people, waiting to be unlocked. People want to be engaged in what they do. If employers build the foundation, employees will do the rest.
>
> —From *MAGIC: Five Keys to Unlock the Power of Employee Engagement*

The idea of handing a stranger the keys to the front door of your home sounds a little fishy. Even with a quick email introduction, renting out your apartment on the Internet for a few days to some guy you've never met challenges common sense. But it's an even greater stretch to set up an entire company based on the idea that you could entice millions of people to rent out their private abodes to strangers. But that's exactly what "sharing economy" superstar Airbnb did, becoming the largest lodging provider on the planet and earning it the title of *Inc.* magazine's "Company of the Year."

Admirable as this new, disruptive business model is, it's not why we have a big man-crush on the company. We admire Airbnb because it's the first high-profile unicorn—and one of the first companies, period—to create the position of chief employee experience officer.

The exact title is global head of employee experience, but you get the gist. Since that time, we've noticed a number of business cards claiming similar titles. Creating such a position legitimizes the growing importance of the Employee Experience, or EX, to organizational success. Not just in a corporate setting, mind you, but in healthcare, academia, the nonprofit sector, and even professional sports.

If you hail from the command-and-control, "All that our employees should expect from us is a paycheck!" school of business, you might be tempted to dismiss chief employee experience officer as a glorified title for the person in charge of Hawaiian Shirt Fridays and foosball tournaments. That would be a mistake. As reported by *Forbes*:

> At Airbnb we are focused on bringing to life our mission of creating a world where you can #belonganywhere, by creating

memorable workplace experiences which span all aspects of how we relate to employees.[1]

That thinking reflects the new reality of which many organizational leaders are just becoming aware. The long-sought "secret sauce" of rising profits, stellar customer satisfaction, and sustainable growth has one key ingredient: an outstanding EX. For decades, executives and managers have sweated in their corporate kitchens, trying to cook up profits and growth by blending together every imaginable ingredient of the organizational recipe.

They've radically redesigned products and rolled out one innovation after another. They've implemented extensive survey and customer satisfaction measurement systems, mined data for possible insights, and reached out to customers with terabytes of personalized messages and offers. They've slashed costs and waved around discounts. And, with a few exceptions, most of those efforts have died an expensive death—and taken a few careers to the grave with them.

Meanwhile, other organizations (including a few we'll highlight in this book) chug along quietly, building transformational workforces, and surpassing their goals year after year because they understand something that's just now becoming evident to their less successful counterparts:

> Every important business outcome lies downstream from the experience and engagement of the people who make the organization go.

This is a bold claim, and we stand by every word. Time and time again, we have found that every business outcome has its root in an individual or a group of people. This observation has led us to realize that success does not begin with a spreadsheet, a slogan, or even a piece of game-changing technology. Success begins and ends with human beings.

That's what the EX is about: creating an operating environment that inspires your people to do great things.

EMPLOYEE ENGAGEMENT

With all due respect, we picked up on this concept a while ago. Our firm, DecisionWise, has been leading the "employee engagement" charge for years. Our database of tens of millions of employee survey responses shows an unmistakable correlation between how deeply employees are engaged in their work and everything from retention to revenue growth to customer satisfaction scores.

The secret is out . . . in some organizations. That's a good thing, because the workforce is changing faster than at any time in history. Until very recently, and despite plenty of evidence to the contrary, most employers clung to the outdated view of employees as interchangeable parts of a business machine. Some have even stopped referring to people by their names and have started calling them "assets" or "human capital." That's not necessarily a bad thing (at least they're starting to understand and see value in the human component of business), but it does tend to highlight the impersonal manner in which organizations see these "assets."

Ego? Stubbornness? It doesn't matter. What matters is that fewer and fewer workers are yoking themselves to the old employee model. They're driving for Uber. They're using tools like Upwork and Thumbtack to become freelancers. They're earning spending money on TaskRabbit and paying the bills with what they make renting out their houses on VRBO (or Airbnb). They're hitting sites like AngelList and Indeed to find open jobs at the hottest startups. They have options they've never had before.

These trends lead us to another important observation:

> Because success starts with talented people, your most important role as a leader is to give them a reason to join your cause, a reason to stay, and a reason to engage.

Don't just take our word for it. Consider what *The Future of Work* author Jacob Morgan wrote in *Forbes*:

> Decades ago nobody cared about the employee experience because all of the power was in the hands of employers. . . . (P)ower has now shifted into the hands of employees.[2]

That's the sound of a microphone dropping. It's also your call to action. Are you ready to challenge the conventional wisdom about what makes an organization great? To stop wasting millions on what doesn't work and do what does—and in the process, create and enjoy your own EX more than you ever thought possible? Good. Keep reading.

ENGAGEMENT MAGIC®

In 2014, we published *MAGIC: Five Keys to Unlock the Power of Employee Engagement.* It was a popular and successful book about our five-part approach to creating engagement in any organization, which goes by the acronym MAGIC:

- **M**eaning
- **A**utonomy
- **G**rowth
- **I**mpact
- **C**onnection

In that book, we wrote a great deal about the theory and methodology of employee engagement. While it was important to establish the way in which engagement can be fostered within organizations, we also realized that for our next book we needed to take readers to a different level: We needed to tell them how to create MAGIC within their companies, schools, hospitals, or nonprofits.

The reason is that employee engagement has never been something leaders can create by decree. You don't roll in a few arcade games, start onsite Pilates classes, hand out environmentally friendly employee handbooks, and announce, "Hey, everybody! We are now an engaged company!" Engagement grows organically from a fertile soil of culture, purposeful work, respect, and trust. As a leader, you can introduce initiatives designed to promote meaning, autonomy, and more in the workplace (and we'll spotlight some organizations that have done exactly that). But whether the seeds of engagement take root is out of your hands.

In approaching *The Employee Experience*, we saw that while we had told organizations *what* MAGIC was, we needed to tell them *how* to make MAGIC happen and *how* to create that authentic engagement that drives success. But by what means? Remember, engagement is a choice. Organizational leaders don't decide if engagement happens; employees do.

It occurred to us that while we couldn't offer a simple, plug-and-play engagement how-to system, we could teach executives, managers, supervisors, department heads, and directors the HR equivalent of tilling the soil, fertilizing, weeding, and watering—creating the right conditions under which engagement can, and will, flourish. So that's what we've done.

BEYOND ENGAGEMENT MAGIC

Since releasing *MAGIC*, we've been knee-deep in additional extensive research, including adding over 10 million responses to the 14 million responses already in our massive employee survey database. That's a lot of data. When we took a closer look at that data, we saw a clear pattern: The most engaged organizations were those where leaders took the greatest care to manage employee expectations and build trust. Even if work was demanding or times were hard, employees always felt like they were dealt with honestly, openly, and respectfully. Values and expectations were aligned. Accusations of broken promises or hypocrisy were rare, if they occurred at all. There was a "band of brothers" feeling that didn't exist in other, less successful organizations. These organizations flourished.

That insight led to this book. In order to engineer an organization infused with MAGIC, you have to create an environment in which employees feel comfortable investing in your mission. That's a risk, and they'll only take it if they believe the organization will fulfill the expectations that were created when they signed on, in keeping with past promises and shared values.

The Employee Experience is our user's manual for creating an environment where MAGIC will thrive. In it, we reveal the three critical components of a superlative EX:

1. Expectation Alignment
2. The Three Contracts
3. Trust

We also reveal how they work and why. These are the key ingredients of a great EX, and when you have them in place, engagement will inevitably follow.

One more thing: From time to time, we've pulled out our old university mortarboards, blown off the dust, and gotten our academic on. You can see us go full nerd in the sidebars called "Egghead Alerts," a popular feature from our last book that we've repeated here. In Egghead Alerts, we'll get into exhaustive (and possibly, exhausting) detail on industrial-organizational psychology concepts that we feel relate to the topic at hand. If that stuff interests you, take a minute to read them. If not, skip them. We won't know. No harm, no foul.

OUR GOALS

We're tired of watching organizations hemorrhage talented people while wasting resources on employee satisfaction measures that just aren't that important. We're sick of seeing companies spend billions on marketing, Big Data, and other means of winning customer love and loyalty while ignoring what makes a great Customer Experience (CX): the EX. It's time for all that to change.

Relying on plenty of real-world examples and lots of our own data, we explain the three components of a transformative EX in detail. In the process, we're going to reveal a powerful, hidden behavioral and psychological dimension to your organization that few people know about, and show you how to master it. When you understand Expectation Alignment (EA), the Contracts, and Trust, and when you possess the tools to shape and use them with intention, you'll create a culture in which a superlative EX can take root. Do that, and MAGIC flourishes and takes care of itself—as do retention, customer satisfaction, profitability, and growth.

We have one overarching goal: stronger organizations. That means better companies, teams, hospitals, schools, churches, communities, teams, volunteer organizations . . . you name it. Regardless of the scope of the organization, we want our readers to enjoy success. Not just financial success, but category-redefining, sustainable, innovative, best-company-on-the-block success. We want you to become experts in the Employee Experience and drive a new era in which employees are not simply easily replaceable labor but partners in creating something extraordinary. When you look at the organizations we feature in these chapters, you'll see that's precisely what some have done. They have redefined how they think about expectations and trust, what they owe their employees, and what their employees owe them.

Frankly, our goal is to give you an unfair advantage over your competition: attracting, keeping, and growing people who make your organization better and your customers happier.

Enough prelude. Let's get busy.

—Tracy Maylett, Ed.D.
Matthew Wride, J.D.
Utah, USA

Acronyms

Throughout this book, we will use a number of acronyms and abbreviations. We've included some of these below to give you a head start.

CX: Customer Experience

EA: Expectation Alignment

EAD: Expectation Alignment Dysfunction

ELC: Employee Life Cycle

EVP: Employee Value Proposition

EX: Employee Experience

HR: Human Resources

MAGIC: Meaning, Autonomy, Growth, Impact, Connection

MOT: Moment of Truth

Great Expectations

CHAPTER 1

You're Digging in the Wrong Place

Everyone thinks of changing the world, but no one thinks of changing himself.

—LEO TOLSTOY

The customer. It's any person or group receiving a service from an individual or organization. If you run a company, it's the person buying your T-shirts, pizza, or software. In healthcare, it's the patient. In education, it's the student. The customer in a not-for-profit may be the child in a remote village who receives food and medical care. In any case, the customer is the reason every organization exists—the reason people have a job to come to. So why are so many organizations (and people) doing such a terrible job giving the customer a wonderful experience?

We're not talking about *you*, of course. Or maybe we are. Because most organizations have the same problem: They are desperate to win their customers' loyalty and affection, but don't know how to do it. Bribery with discounts doesn't work. Innovation doesn't work, because their competitors just out-innovate them. So they spend fortunes and waste years fishing for something that does work—and usually fail.

Still, a comparatively few organizations are getting it right. They win their customers' loyalty and affection. They build brands that seem impervious to harm. What's their secret? It's right in front of them, and it's right in front of you, too. It's your *employees.* They are the secret to thrilled customers who boost profits, provide referrals, and who keep coming back. The trouble is, you're probably not treating your employees as though this were true. We're going to show you how to change that and, in the process, change everything.

But first, it's time for a gratuitous pop culture reference.

CX (NOT INDIANA JONES) IS KING

If you read our book *MAGIC: Five Keys to Unlock the Power of Employee Engagement*, you know we're not above using examples from TV or movies to make a point. In that book, we cited the film *Office Space* as a memorable example of a completely disengaged workplace. At the risk of going to that particular well once too often, join us for a brief interlude in Cairo, the setting for an early part of the classic film *Raiders of the Lost Ark*.

In the scene, Indiana Jones and his friend Sallah have taken the golden headpiece of the Staff of Ra to a white-haired mystic, hoping he can decipher markings that will lead them to the Ark of the Covenant. When the old man translates the markings into instructions for the staff's height, Indy and Sallah realize simultaneously that the staff the Nazis are using in their search is too long, thus giving them inaccurate information about the location of the Ark. They look at each other delightedly and in unison utter the memorable line: "They're digging in the wrong place."

When we began writing this book, we couldn't get that phrase out of our heads. As we've watched hundreds of organizations obsess over Customer Experience (CX) and burn billions in their efforts, we couldn't help but think "They're digging in the wrong place." It's not that CX isn't important; on the contrary, it's absolutely crucial to profitability and growth. In fact, a 2015 report from Forrester illustrates this unambiguously.[1] According to the findings, a one-point improvement in an industry's Average CX Index™ Score is worth huge revenue increases to the companies within that sector.

We're talking about $65 million in extra annual revenue for an upscale hotel chain, $118 million for a luxury auto brand, and a whopping $175 million a year in new revenues for a wireless service provider. To drive the point home, look at *Harvard Business Review*'s analysis, which asserts that a 1.3 percent improvement in customer satisfaction scores equals a 0.5 percent jump in revenue.[2]

No wonder everybody's talking about the Customer Experience. You probably are. Your organization might even mention your commitment to improving CX on your website or in your mission statement. It makes sense, and we agree. Your customers should be the focus of your business, because without them, you don't have a business. Sam Walton of Walmart fame said it best: "There is only one boss. The customer. And he can fire everybody in the company from the chairman on down, simply by spending his money somewhere else." That's precisely the reason so many organizations are putting so much time and effort into redefining and redesigning the Customer Experience.

> Despite customer satisfaction being rocket fuel for the bottom line, organizations are burning billions in fruitless efforts to create a profit-boosting CX.

YOU CAN'T GET THERE FROM HERE

Intuitively, each of us understands what it means to be disappointed by a poor Customer Experience or delighted by the employee who goes above and beyond the call. Given the potential upside, dumping man-hours and resources into CX seems like the no-brainer of all time. But is it, really? Can you engineer a superlative CX by throwing resources directly at the customer or by demanding that your downtrodden employees deliver service with a smile? Is it that simple?

Corporate leaders certainly seem to think so. One 2014 report forecasts that the market for CX management services and technology will grow from $4.36 billion in 2015 to $10.77 billion by 2020.[3] That's real money. Companies are spending lavishly on comprehensive CX strategies and building or buying high-tech systems in order to mine what they see as untapped veins of growth. And the data insist that this preoccupation with CX is justified: A report by the American Customer Satisfaction Index showed that leaders in customer service outperformed the Dow by 93 percent, the Fortune 500 by 20 percent, and the NASDAQ by a whopping 335 percent.[4]

However, the methods that many organizations are using to try to duplicate those glowing figures just aren't delivering. According to *The Consumer Conversation* report, only 37 percent of businesses surveyed said they were "able to tie customer experience activities to revenue and/or cost savings."[5] That means the majority are, in effect, just spending money and keeping their fingers crossed. Meanwhile, an Accenture report concluded that, despite ambitious plans, about half the surveyed companies' CX initiatives actually did little or nothing to retain customers or grow global revenues.[6]

What about outside the traditional corporate world, say, in healthcare? The news there is no better. A survey by PricewaterhouseCoopers of more than 2,300 healthcare patients found that only half were satisfied with their overall experience as healthcare consumers. Ominously (for insurance companies, anyway), many were willing to try nontraditional sources for health insurance, including large retailers (40 percent of respondents) and digital companies like Amazon (37 percent).[7]

Despite customer satisfaction being rocket fuel for the bottom line, organizations are burning billions in unproductive efforts to create a profit-boosting CX. That's what we mean by "digging in the wrong place."

THROWING YOUR EMPLOYEES UNDER THE BUS

Consider the Chicago Transit Authority (CTA). In 2013, the CTA spent $454 million to transition its 1.7 million daily riders from its own proprietary fare collection system to a third-party system owned and developed by a company called Ventra.[8] But rather than saving money and time, the CTA only succeeded in enraging tens of thousands of Chicagoans.

The CTA's mistake was that it focused on improving CX by increasing efficiency but did so without taking into account its employees—you know, the people who best knew its customers' behavior, who knew that they were happy with the current system, and who would be on the front lines of customer anger and frustration. It was a costly miscalculation.

For example, buses were redesigned so that riders boarding through the front door would be automatically charged by electronic sensors as they passed by. No swiping cards—great, right? Sure, until you realize that on a crowded city bus, riders tend to use the fastest, most convenient exit. Unfortunately, the CTA didn't talk to its bus drivers before installing the expensive system. If it had, it would have learned that many riders also exit through the front door. After the new system came online, many riders were inadvertently charged twice. Whoops.

Technical problems plagued the new system, and the CTA dropped the ball by making customer service available only between 7 a.m. and 8 p.m. on weekdays. Since many people ride the trains and buses in the evenings and on weekends, this decision left huge swaths of time that passengers couldn't get help from a real person. In some cases, the customer service issues were tragicomic, including the experience of one passenger who started getting email after email telling him his new Ventra card was on the way, followed by a blizzard of mail: 91 envelopes, each containing a new card. The comedy of errors didn't stop there. "The next day, 176 more [cards] arrived, each one, he later discovered, canceling the last. 'You have to call and activate it,' the rider told *Crain's Chicago Business*, 'but I've been afraid to do that.'"[9]

Eventually, the CTA had to go back to selling its former magnetic stripe cards while it figured out what went wrong, which was something its employees could have pointed out before the costly move to a new system.[10] Meanwhile, as riders became more and more fed up and indignant, the agency threw its employees—pardon the pun—under the bus. In December 2013, one call center worker lost her job after the *Chicago Tribune* published a letter in which a frustrated customer recounted his repeated attempts to get a Ventra card. But customer support calls were routed to a call center in San Francisco, so call center workers had no firsthand knowledge of the city or the system. The sacked worker was merely the last service rep the customer had spoken to, and she had been working for eleven days straight. Nevertheless, she was sent packing—on her birthday—for "bringing bad press to Ventra."[11]

The CTA's greatest blunder wasn't choosing faulty technology or dealing with incompetent partners to fix a system that wasn't broken. It was failing to work with its greatest asset, its employees, to understand and improve its Customer Experience.

DIGGING IN THE RIGHT PLACE

It's clear that in the quest for a stellar CX and the profits it yields, we have become seduced by the hype without really understanding what creates a positive revenue and service-enhancing Customer Experience in the first place.

Part of the problem is that there isn't even agreement on how to gauge CX's impact. How can you directly attribute growth or revenue increases to an improved Customer Experience? By definition, the term is a catchall for every interaction the customer has with an organization: first contact with a company's website, an interaction with the clerk at the Department of Motor Vehicles, or your wait in the emergency room while your weeping child cradles her injured wrist. Who's to say that one small sliver of the overall CX—caring service by a kind and helpful call center service rep, for example—might not be responsible for 80 percent of a company's CX-related revenue spike, rendering the other CX measures mostly meaningless? Teasing out cause and effect can be maddening.

So we're not going to try. Instead, we're going to dig somewhere else and introduce you to a company that's been doing things differently. Back in 2002, healthcare staffing firm CHG Healthcare Services was average. Growth rates were average. Sales and revenue figures were average. Employee turnover was—you guessed it—average. But the executive team had no interest in simply being average.

CHG wanted to be the largest and best healthcare staffing company in the country. However, its lukewarm corporate culture was restricting growth, and its turnover rate of 48 percent made it virtually impossible to hire and train employees fast enough to grow substantially. At that time, the CHG culture was similar to that of most companies: Communication was mostly top-down, divisional cultures differed, and HR focused on general administrative practices. It was a "good place to work," but few employees were passionate about what they did.

CHG's transformation started as an initiative to reduce turnover by understanding the issues that caused it. Leaders chose to focus on the value of their people, which led to a "Putting People First" program. They also decided to collect feedback from their employees and implemented an annual employee engagement survey, among other sources of communication. The feedback from employees was sometimes painful for the executive team to hear, but it provided many opportunities for improvement.

Gradually, CHG built a culture of feedback. Accountability and trust improved. Employees knew that their feedback was heard and acted upon. Today, CHG's leaders regard the company's employees as its strategic advantage. "Putting People First" is the defining organizational value, and it influences every decision. Employees rave about how much they love their jobs. CHG is at the top of our list of engaged organizations and has ranked as high as number 3 on *Fortune* magazine's "100 Best Companies to Work For" list, in the same league as titans like Google and SAS.

During the weekend following the announcement that CHG had taken the number 3 spot on the *Fortune* list, dozens of employees were so proud of the accomplishment that they gathered for the better part of a Saturday—unbeknownst to management—to record a YouTube music video entitled "Three Is Our Magic Number."[12] For CHG, "Putting People First" was more than just a catchy phrase that served as a clever double entendre to their missions of placing candidates in healthcare positions and taking care of employees. Engaged employees, who were clearly the top priority at CHG, created engaging Customer Experiences.

As for results, CHG is the most profitable company in the healthcare staffing industry. Turnover has dropped to less than half the industry average, and the company even managed to grow revenue and profits during the 2008 to 2011 recession while industry peers saw profitability plummet. CHG knew where to dig.

EX = CX

Organizations like CHG understand that you can't build a transformative Customer Experience directly, solely by throwing resources at CX initiatives. You can redesign stores, roll out cool new products, and engage customers on social media; there's nothing wrong with those steps. But without employees who care about customer service, a beautiful store is just a pretty shell. Without people incented to take risks, where are those cool innovations coming from? Don't even get us started on the dangers of having jaded or clueless staffers meeting customers on Twitter. In other words:

> To create a sustainable, world-class CX, an organization must first create a sustainable, world-class Employee Experience (EX).

It all begins with your employees. In the next few pages we'll define what we mean by EX, and we'll lay out a framework to build the right EX for your organization. For now, think of it this way. Creating a wonderful, profit-boosting CX is like gardening. You can't order up the results you want—healthy plants—just by waving your hand. Gardening is a process-based activity; you attend to the components that create the desired outcome and then hope for the best. That means using soil amendments, watering, and weeding. The gardener can't do much more than that, but if he or she does it well, the odds of a strong, plentiful harvest are high.

Growing an organization works in the same way. Success comes through quality products, sensible pricing, strong customer support . . . and employees who care personally about delivering an extraordinary experience every time. When an organization creates a top-notch EX, the likelihood of a superior CX increases exponentially. When EX is poor, chances are the customer will see the effects. So, here's the bottom line:

EX = CX

Your employees are the soil and nutrients in which your Customer Experience grows. If you have a workforce of engaged people who feel respected and appreciated, and if they trust their leaders enough to take risks and invest emotionally in the organization, your CX will take care of itself.

Conversely, if you don't have that foundation of great people who care about providing a terrific experience and making customers' lives better, all the technology and systems in the world won't keep your CX from being a money-losing mess.

Engaged employees are the soil and nutrients in which your Customer Experience grows.

CONGRUENT EXPERIENCE

Despite this, too many organizations try to dash past EX in favor of CX. Why doesn't it work? For starters, CX is an *outcome.* For decades, managers have treated customer satisfaction as though it were something they could conjure out of procedures, perks, and pricing. Wrong. That's like deciding to lose twenty pounds by taking weight loss pills while ignoring a healthy diet and exercise. Even if you get results, they won't last—and you will waste a lot of money in the process.

A winning CX is the direct result of the attitudes and behaviors of your employees. Employees should come first, with results to follow, not the other way around. Think of it this way: When you went through your most recent customer service trauma, did you ask yourself: "What type of experience are we providing for the employee(s) who were involved in the problem?" Probably not. But was the crisis a direct result of someone failing to step up to keep a promise, identify and resolve a concern, or provide one small extra bit of service? We'll bet it was. The point? For most organizations, their awareness of the EX does not match up with the important role it plays in determining the CX.

Employees are the face of your brand. They're on the front lines and in direct contact with your customers. Sure, customers are also seeing your website, marketing, and real estate, but those do not outweigh a salesperson who goes out of her way to solve a problem or a school counselor who stays late to help a student with college scholarship forms. Consumers are human, and humans intuitively respond to human interactions more than they do slogans, packaging, or discounts.

That's why the Employee Experience (EX) has far more potential than the CX to move the needle for your organization, by whatever metric you choose: revenue, growth, retention, customer satisfaction scores, number of students registered, patient satisfaction, and so on. But putting EX before CX also serves as a way to prevent your organization from diving down expensive, time-consuming rabbit holes.

Think about the costs, financial and otherwise, of implementing a CX management program where employees' hearts and minds aren't fully engaged. Some organizations spend a fortune on elaborate customer service safety nets designed to keep employees from damaging the customer relationship. Why? *Because their employees don't care.* They're having a lousy experience, so they're not motivated to provide anything more than that to the customer. We call this the Law of Congruent Experience.

THE LAW OF CONGRUENT EXPERIENCE

Employees will deliver a Customer Experience that matches their own experience in the organization.

Indifferent employees mean indifferent customers. Angry employees put in minimal effort to take care of the customer. Customers respond in kind. In contrast, employees who are engaged and trust their employers will provide a great CX because they *choose* to. You don't need call scripts or a patients' bill of rights to keep them from damaging your brand. You can turn them loose, knowing that they will solve problems on their own, increase value, and breed customer loyalty. A terrific EX equals a superb, loyalty-winning, profit-creating CX.

DEFINING THE EMPLOYEE EXPERIENCE

We've been clear that in order to create a superior CX, an organization needs to first take care of its EX. But what, exactly, is the "Employee Experience"?

Some mistakenly confuse the EX with popular terms like "Talent Management," "Human Resources Development," or "Employee Engagement." While EX is certainly related to those terms, it's not synonymous with them. EX is much broader in scope. So, for our purposes, here's how we define EX:

> The Employee Experience is the sum of perceptions employees have about their interactions with the organization in which they work.

In the introduction to this book, we mentioned a trend leading many HR executives (and even marketing departments) to take on titles like "Chief Employee Experience Officer." On one hand, it's wonderful to see because it makes us think they get it. But then we ask them to describe what "Employee Experience" means, and they bring out charts and models that are really describing the Employee Life Cycle (ELC).

While it certainly is a part of EX, the ELC is distinct, made up of all the steps or processes in which an employee participates during his or her relationship with the organization. An ELC is chronological and sequential, and assumes a beginning and an end. For example, the ELC includes important events and processes like recruiting, onboarding, employee development, promotion, and exit interviews. The ELC is an important part of the human resources process, because it takes into account the steps that occur from an employee's first contact with the organization to the last interaction after termination. However, the ELC differs from the EX in two very significant ways: *perceptions* and *expectations.*

Consider this. Two friends, Ingvar and Edvar, start new jobs on the same day with the same company. For the first year, they are assigned to the same boss, work in the same manufacturing facility, and have similar job responsibilities. Their compensation is identical. In fact, nearly every step of the ELC is identical. Yet their EX is very different.

Ingvar has two children, both involved in football. When he joined the company, one of the things he found most attractive was that the company touted the importance of work-life balance, which was important to him because he wanted to support his children's athletic events. Edvar is single. He's all about the late-night party scene, so he finds getting to work before 9:00 in the morning (at least with a clear head) challenging, particularly on the nights he plays guitar in the band.

Fortunately for Ingvar, the company has some flexibility in how early employees leave in the afternoon, as long as they begin at 7:00 a.m. sharp and finish critical projects before heading out for the day. Ingvar finds this a real plus. Edvar, however, feels constrained by the 7:00 a.m. start time. It simply doesn't meet his needs. He also thought that "work-life balance" meant he would have some flexibility that facilitated the "life" part of the equation as much as it did the "work" part. No such luck. In fact, last time he brought it up to his supervisor, he was told to "go read the policy manual." He had also understood that he could be fast-tracked to a management position if he showed promise, which, in his mind, he clearly has. But he's still in the same role he was in when he started with Ingvar over a year ago. He begins looking for new employment.

Two employees. Identical ELC experiences. Very different EXs.

EX depends largely on perception and expectations. (We'll cover the expectations part in more depth in the next chapter.) The perception portion dictates the outcome of the experience. The EX is based on the employee's perception of what it going on, not always on the reality of what occurs. This is why Ingvar and Edvar can have identical experiences yet their EXs can be vastly different:

EX = Experiences + Expectations + Perceptions

A positive EX, then, isn't just a factor of what the company throws at the employee. Rather, it's a result of how the employee perceives those experiences, and whether or not they meet her expectations.

Most organizations fail to understand this concept. They believe that creating a stellar EX is a matter of tossing out a few perks that they believe to be universally appealing (seriously, who doesn't like Taco

EGGHEAD ALERT!

Field Theory

Developed by psychologist Kurt Lewin, the concepts of "life space" and "field theory" are now important parts of social and organizational psychology. Lewin taught that behavior (B) is a function (f) of personal (P) and environmental (E) factors:

$$B = f(PE)$$

Lewin defined "life space" as a combination of the factors that influence an individual at any point in time. These factors could include life experience, memories, needs, personality, health, desires, and others. As these factors differ from person to person, each individual's life space differs from that of another individual. The field, then, is the environment that exists in the individual's (or group's) mind. This field changes over time and with experiences. Field theory explains why two individuals (or groups) may encounter a nearly identical situation but may interpret that situation differently.

Tuesdays or a tube slide from the third floor down to the lobby?), then calling themselves "great places to work." Yet their workers are still unhappy, and they move on to places where their EX is better aligned with what they're looking for. After all, in today's environment, employees have choices.

ENLIGHTENED SELF-INTEREST

In our definition of EX, we aren't simply trying to capture how an employee "feels" about the organization. EX is broader in scope. We are looking at whether an organization's EX attracts the right people and then provides them with an environment that helps them do their best work. In turn, this results in success for the organization. Your job as a leader is to design, build, and maintain the right EX so that the sum of your employees' perceptions, whether across your organization, division, or team, encourages and produces the very best in your people.

We're not advocating that you create a workers' utopia or spend all your resources making workers happier. Just because employees are happy doesn't mean they're performing at a high level. Employee engagement is about people doing meaningful work in a way that makes them feel that they are growing and their expectations are being met. Difficult, challenging, and even exhausting work can be engaging—and employees can love doing it—if you as the leader create a framework that understands and meets people's expectations and rewards their contributions.

For instance, teaching is one of the most grueling professions around: long hours, budget cuts, pressure from parents and administrators, and the monumental challenge of trying to shape young minds of all backgrounds and aptitudes. Talk to teachers and it's rare to find one who doesn't find the work draining—and most would never do anything else. Teaching always ranks on the annual *Forbes* list of happiest jobs. Why? Meaning and impact (two of our MAGIC keys). For these teachers, their EX is exactly what they wanted. For many, teaching is also connected to *enlightened self-interest,* where serving others is, ultimately, good for oneself as well.

Having engaged employees is good for your company, school, or nonprofit. An engaged workforce translates to high customer satisfaction scores, high customer loyalty, stronger growth, better patient care, and higher profits. It means lower turnover and lower recruitment costs. It even means less workplace stress and reduced healthcare costs. Our own research, as well as studies by other researchers, shows that that engaged employees lead healthier lifestyles, have fewer chronic health issues, and are more likely to get involved in company wellness programs.[13] If employees are also happier, smile more, and have better personal lives, that's a bonus (and not an insignificant one).

A great example of this is SSL encryption (the link between your web browser and servers that safeguards your private information) company DigiCert. When you call DigiCert for support, you won't be transferred. Every phone support person is empowered to solve your problem from beginning to end and has discretion to make refunds or award billing credits. DigiCert built its business on web security, search engine optimization, and crazy-good customer support. It doesn't do much additional marketing because it doesn't need to. The company mantra is that you should never put the customer on hold or tell them you will call them back. Employees strive to solve all support issues on the first call.

DigiCert employees love this, and the company treats them like gold, including paying for an annual vacation. In fact, many employees won't even think of leaving, partly because they can't imagine losing their "DigiTrip." You might think that the company perked its way to an engaged workforce, but that's not it. This is a company culture based on empowerment and service. Employees are loving their EX, so they make sure their customers do, too. Everybody wins.

Oh yeah, DigiCert has been on Deloitte's Fast 500 list, which ranks the fastest-growing North American companies in the technology, media, telecommunications, life sciences, and energy tech sectors, every year since 2010. So, do you think this approach is working for the company?

> Difficult, challenging, and even exhausting work can be engaging if you create a framework that understands and meets people's expectations and rewards their contributions.

THE AGE OF THE EMPLOYEE

People agree to give their time and energy to their employer hoping for such exemplary, or at least reciprocal, treatment. They trust that the employer will reward them for their hard work, give them a reasonable degree of job security, and fulfill reasonable expectations—basically, keep its word. So it seems like common sense that employers should take reasonable steps to create a fulfilling and engaging EX, right?

Unfortunately, we don't live in that ideal world. Historically, the employer-employee relationship has been more adversarial than collaborative. In general, employees assumed that companies would exploit them and break every promise they made, while employers regarded employees as liabilities and layabouts who, if given an inch, would take a mile, cheating and stealing as they went. Ouch.

That model, however, is changing. Some leaders haven't figured it out yet, but we're already in the Age of the Employee. This doesn't mean that employees have all the power. They simply have more options than ever. That means it is harder to find and keep those employees who might be the difference between slow, struggling growth and sector-leading celebrity.

Progress stalled during the recession that began in 2008 because people were afraid to leave their jobs for greener pastures. But with the world economy improving, employees are feeling empowered. Indeed.com, the world's largest employment website, released the results of a 2016 study that showed 50 percent of U.S. workers thinking about making a career change.[14] And we're seeing similar sentiment throughout much of the world. That's tens (or hundreds) of millions of people feeling pretty confident about their skills and opportunities. They're feeling that way because they know that talent, not capital, is the difference-making resource in any organization.

Sir Richard Branson gets it. The mercurial Virgin Group founder, who famously got his first taste of the aviation business when he and his wife were stranded in Puerto Rico and he chartered a plane to carry himself and other passengers home, puts his employees before his customers. Branson believes that it should go without saying that when employees are proud of their jobs, are given the right tools, and are looked after, the result is a positive customer experience. In an interview with *Inc.*, he explains why:

> [My] philosophy has always been, if you can put staff first, your customer second, and shareholders third, effectively, in the end, the shareholders do well, the customers do better, and [you,] yourself are happy.[15]

As we mentioned, during the past five years we have gathered more than 24 million employee survey responses—the largest database of its kind—in order to understand the relationship between the Employee Experience and the Customer Experience. This research shows that, while most would say they are engaged in their jobs, only a small minority of employees consider themselves "fully engaged" at work. Turns out that those entrenched policies that treated employees like interchangeable parts who were lucky to have a job in the first place were terrible for morale, retention, and customer satisfaction. Scary thought if you're relying on those people to manufacture your pacemaker or teach your child.

Try this exercise. Imagine that someone asked you about your organization right now. Where would you begin your story? Its history, maybe? Revenue growth? Number of students enrolled in your programs? Average patient wait times? Market share? You probably wouldn't start by talking about your employees. You're not alone. When we look at the engines that drive organizations to success, the people who make things go every day are usually an afterthought.

That's backward and dead wrong, morally and fiscally. After years of genuflecting before the customer while treating employees as expendable, we're finally starting to see that we've been watering the leaves, not the roots, of our organizations. If you want an extraordinary business, hospital, nonprofit, school, church, or sports team, you need an extraordinary EX that creates that band-of-brothers feeling and makes people feel cared about, inspired, and respected.

YOUR PEOPLE ARE YOUR BRAND

Since we're on the edge of corporate blasphemy, let's jump in with both feet. What we're really talking about is your brand: what your organization stands for and how it makes people feel. Brand is the Holy Grail of business; we're always growing, maintaining, repairing, or defending it. But your employees *create* it.

Not your marketing department. Not PR. Not products. If your brand is a promise, then your employees are responsible for keeping that promise. If you have fully engaged employees who care about making customers happy, you can have a second-rate logo, an out-of-date website, and awkward advertising and not dent your brand. Just ask the employees at Men's Wearhouse, the discount suit chain that thrived despite cheesy TV ads featuring founder George Zimmer saying "I guarantee it" and has floundered ever since Zimmer's board forced him out in 2013. Many would argue Zimmer's belief that employees (tailors, in particular) come first also left with him.[16]

Your employees are your brand. It lives through the performance, interactions, and genuine care of the people who bring it to life on the front lines every day. We're not saying that you shouldn't work on building an exemplary Customer Experience; that would be bad practice. We're simply asking you to do it in a different way, understanding the most important factor in shaping that experience: the people on your payroll.

In other words, start digging in the right place. Let's talk about how.

CHAPTER 1. YOU'RE DIGGING IN THE WRONG PLACE: THE CHAPTER EXPERIENCE

- Organizations are digging in the wrong place for an outstanding Customer Experience (CX). It's found by first building an exceptional Employee Experience (EX).
- The Employee Experience is the sum of perceptions employees have about their interactions with the organization in which they work.
- Customer satisfaction clearly impacts profits, but you can't create it directly.
- Employees know more about what customers want than anyone; understand that and use it.
- Fostering feedback, transparency, respect, and appreciation improves engagement, retention, and the bottom line.
- You can have a transformational CX only if you first have a transformational EX.
- The Law of Congruent Experience: Employees will give customers an experience that reflects their own.
- EX is not about making employees happy, but about fostering engagement that grows your bottom line.
- We're in an era (The Age of the Employee) when employees have more choices and influence than ever.
- Your employees are your brand.

CHAPTER 2

The Expectation Gap

Blessed are they who expect nothing for they shall not be disappointed.

—L.M. Montgomery, *Anne of Green Gables*

In 1960, a German company called B.N.S. International Sales Corporation sold a shipment of chickens to Frigaliment Importing Company. But when the chickens arrived, Frigaliment found that they were older, lower-quality "stewing hens," not the higher quality "broiler chickens" it had expected. Frigaliment sued B.N.S. for breach of contract (technically, breach of warranty), claiming that B.N.S. was obligated to provide the specific types of chickens described in their contract.

In district court, a judge dismissed the complaint, in part because while Frigaliment claimed that "chicken" always means "broiler chickens," in German, the word can mean either kind of chicken. The definition of the word was ambiguous, so the contract could not be enforced.[1]

That's a classic case that's studied as part of every law school curriculum. We bring it up to illustrate the impact that establishing, meeting, or violating expectations has on relationships. This was a classic case of one side having expectations based on incomplete information and the other unintentionally violating those expectations. When that happens, matters often wind up in severed relationships or even litigation. Litigation exists because one side in an agreement fails—deliberately or inadvertently—to meet the expectations of the other.

Whether those expectations are realistic or reasonable may matter when it comes to the resolution of litigation, but it has little bearing on whether one party chooses to *initiate* litigation. Expectations aren't always rational, nor do logic and evidence always play the chief roles in shaping them. Perhaps the only thing each party would agree to in this case would be that nobody's expectations were aligned.

Consider another famous law school case, *Hawkins v. McGee* (New Hampshire, 1929), also known as the "hairy hand case." George Hawkins's hand had been scarred nine years earlier when he tried to turn on a light in his family's kitchen. Dr. Edward R. B. McGee reached out to Hawkins's father about fixing the hand and guaranteed "a one hundred percent good hand." Unfortunately, McGee used skin from Hawkins's chest for a skin graft, and the palm of Hawkins's new hand wound up sprouting hair. (Insert your own punchline here.) A court awarded Hawkins "expectation damages" based on the difference between what he was promised ("a one hundred percent good hand") and what he received.[2]

TRYING TO PREDICT THE FUTURE

As human beings on a one-way journey through time, we're always trying to peer into the future and choose our actions based on what we expect that future to look like. We base those expectations on a broad range of factors, from the logical (personal experience, hard data, trends, reputation) to the irrational (false information, astrology, gut feel, wishful thinking). We choose to act—or not act—in a certain way because we expect that behavior to produce the outcome that we find most favorable. But, in the end, we're making a leap of faith across a gap in our knowledge, with our only lifelines to the other side being our faith in the quality of our information and our trust in the people involved.

For example, when a young couple buys their first home, they jump into that gap and commit their life savings based on several expectations:

- Their information about the home's current and future value will be reliable.
- The real estate agent will act on their behalf.
- The property inspection will reveal any problems or potential concerns.
- The sellers will be honest about the property's condition.
- The new home will meet their current and future needs.

Sometimes those expectations pan out; sometimes they don't. But the reality is that even with facts, figures, research, and laws in their corner, the quality of the couple's experience depends largely on whether their expectations were upheld or violated—and if they were realistic in the first place.

EGGHEAD ALERT!

Expectancy Theory

Expectancy theory explains why we are motivated to choose one option over another. The theory was developed by Victor Vroom, and is based on three factors, each of which must be considered when we look at motivation:

1. Valence—The value we place on a potential outcome or reward.
2. Expectancy—Our belief that our efforts will result in achieving the desired outcome.
3. Instrumentality—Whether we believe we will receive promised rewards or not.

TO EXPECT IS HUMAN

Expectations are served up with a side of emotion and healthy dollops of trust issues and feelings of entitlement. That's why the age-old marketing and customer service maxim, "Underpromise and overdeliver," remains in use.

When a business, service provider, or anyone in a give-and-take relationship makes a promise—even an implied promise that comes from a marketing brochure or employee handbook—expectations are set. Human beings are hard-wired to form expectations. And as we noted, when people form expectations, they immediately begin using them to plan for the future: *She said she thought my centerpieces might be done three days before the wedding reception, so that gives me plenty of time to finalize the rest of the decorations.* They bank on the promise (whether actual or perceived) and begin to feel that they have a right to it. They believe they have alignment between what they expect and what will occur.

Add the financial commitments that come with an expectation of performance, stir in beliefs about honesty and how we deserve to be treated, and you have a combustible mix. That's why smart service providers set reasonable, even modest, expectations for their customers and then work to exceed them. They create alignment in the areas most likely to be hot points if expectations are not met or misunderstood. It's why wise employers undersell rewards like bonuses to new hires. They know that an employee who gets a $500 year-end bonus will be delighted if he expected to receive nothing. Service providers know that hell hath no fury like the bride-to-be who finds out her centerpieces will be two days late, even if that's still in plenty of time for the big day.

That leads us to the Expectation-Reaction Triangle, shown in Figure 2.1.

So what if the other party's expectations are unrealistic? Are customers always reasonable? Nope. Do women and men always understand

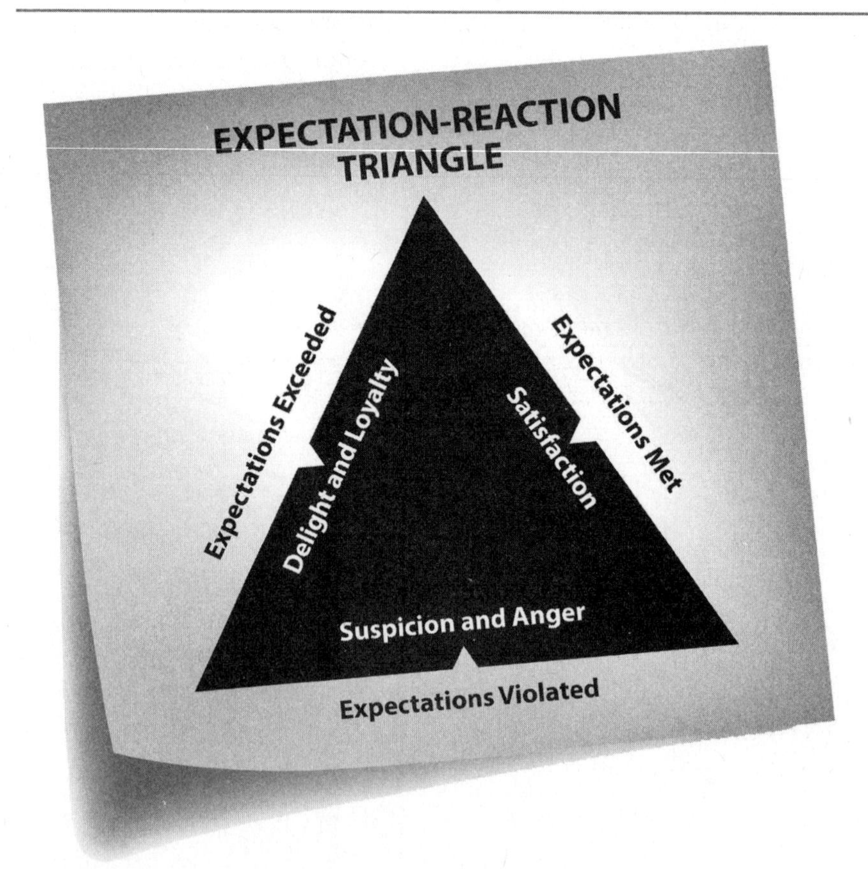

FIGURE 2.1 Expectation-Reaction Triangle

each other? No way. Do employees and employers ever have unreasonable expectations of each other? Sure. The onus is on both parties to monitor, identify, clarify, manage, and, if necessary, push back on expectations. But it's the service provider or employer who carries the brunt of this responsibility.

TURNAROUND

That's rarely truer than it is in public education, where parents' expectations that their children will receive a compassionate, comprehensive education and graduate from high school despite challenges are often at odds with harsh realities. Take Jennings School District, just outside of St. Louis. The compact district of just 3,000 students was a poster child for the ills of an urban, largely minority school system: lots of poverty, lots of conflict, lots of hungry students, and low test scores. In fact, the district's average score of 57 percent on Missouri's standardized tests put the district's accreditation in jeopardy.

Of the myriad challenges a school district like this faces—racism, transferring families, budget cuts, crime—one of the hardest to overcome is apathy: the expectation that kids and their parents can't do any better. As one school board member said, poor districts suffer from the "bigotry of low expectations." If scores and performance get worse, the chasm between what parents expect the schools and teachers to deliver and what teachers and administrators believe students and parents are capable of grows. Cynicism sets in on both sides. Educators start to assume that the situation is hopeless; parents feel betrayed. A death spiral begins as those families who are able to do so pull their kids out of failing districts, which, in turn, lose money and accreditation.

But in 2012, incoming superintendent Tiffany Anderson tackled the low expectations and cynicism by doing something unprecedented: using district resources to alleviate poverty, the social ill underlying most every problem in the schools. She created a district food pantry to address the widespread problem of kids coming to school hungry. She turned a vacant school into a foster home for homeless students and opened a health clinic in Jennings Senior High School so students with health issues could stay at school instead of going to a doctor's office. Most important, she taught teachers to understand the challenges faced by low-income students, not only by providing training in dealing with racism and trauma but also by having teachers live in impoverished conditions for a week.

By 2014, the district's efforts were showing big results: scores up to 78 percent, and 81 percent in 2015, when the district regained its full accreditation. Jennings School District now boasts a 92 percent four-year graduation rate, the result of a team effort between teachers, administrators, parents, and students who had their expectations challenged—and changed.[3]

As Anderson wrote:

> [O]ppression is rooted in practices that contribute to a system becoming self-perpetuating because the conditions are institutionalized and habits are formed that are not interrupted. However, if habits were changed and practices that previously contributed to maintaining impoverished communities were replaced with practices that removed barriers instead of creating them, many more schools nationally would be transformed . . .
>
> . . . The main character in the film *Tomorrowland* described the act of feeding two wolves, one was light and hope and the other was hopelessness and despair. Too often we feed despair and hopelessness and we give rise to the conditions creating hope and despair. The question in the movie was—which wolf are you going to feed?
>
> When I began as superintendent in Jennings in 2012, we chose to feed hope and light resulting in an entire community working together to improve the conditions that give rise to hope and light.[4]

MIND THE GAP!

The experience of the people involved in the Jennings School District is an example of the *Expectation Gap*, the chasm that exists between the expectations created on one side and how people believe their expectations have been met on the other—between what people have been promised and what they *believe* they've been promised.

In Jennings, the school system was weighed down not only by crushing poverty but by the hopelessness it breeds—the assumption by teachers, parents, and just about everyone that nothing would ever change. When Superintendent Anderson's bold programs challenged those expectations, people began to see that they were false. Cynicism began to break down, and change happened.

Every relationship between two or more parties features an Expectation Gap. Whether it's a school, business, marriage, congregation, or community, gaps are a certainty. Sometimes the gap is small. At other times the gap (think broiler chickens and hairy hands) is a mile wide and two miles deep. That gap, when identified and brought to the surface, can serve as an effective impetus for change. As was the case with the school district, the superintendent pointed out the gap between what could be (her expectations) and what was (the reality students, parents, and the community believed to be inevitable). When those involved finally saw the gap's true nature, they identified what it would take to close it.

Let's break down how the Expectation Gap works in an organization. Imagine the company as the two ends of a radio broadcast. The expectation creators operate the transmission tower and send out the broadcast signals. The employees are the individual radio receivers (humor us and pretend that terrestrial radio is still a thing, okay?) on the other end. It might look something like Figure 2.2.

In between the point of transmission and the point of reception lies a gap. The greater the distance from the source, the more the signal begins to deteriorate and fill with static, to the point that it's difficult or impossible over large distances to decipher the original message. This loss of signal strength is why radio stations use repeaters—devices that receive signals, then retransmit those signals—to boost broadcast strength and make sure that even distant listeners get a clear signal.

This gap is common in all organizations, and the distance between expectations and day-to-day experience often grows with poor communication. Remember that the gap is always there to some degree. It's where trust blooms or withers within any organization. Every time authority figures take action or communicate in some way (it doesn't matter if it's an internal newsletter or the CEO getting a new cabin on the lake; everything sends a message), they shoot a signal across the gap that tells employees or subordinates what to expect from the future.

Broadcasts happen 24x7, and each one influences employee expectations about values and brand, culture, pay, the organization's financial

FIGURE 2.2 The Expectation Gap

health, and so on. The trick is making sure that the broadcast signal gets from transmitter to receiver with as much clarity as possible so nobody develops false or insupportable expectations. Therein lies the problem.

SUSAN

Now, let's say we have a new hire named Susan. In the beginning, she's like a radio receiver located just down the street from the transmission tower: She's getting the signal loud and clear (or, at least as clearly as she needs, for the time being). She's just had her onboarding interview, read the employee handbook, and signed an employment contract, so her expectations for things like salary, vacation, bonuses, performance reviews, and the like are unambiguous. Susan is receiving information (the company's expectations for performance) and is also sending information back (her own expectations).

Time passes. As she gains more experience and leaves the orientation phase of her training, Susan moves away from the original source. The signal and reception become sketchy. As with many of her colleagues, the gap between Susan's expectations and what she experiences in her day-to-day work begins to widen. The signal becomes less clear as she relies on her supervisors to relay signals back and forth. This becomes particularly problematic when those "repeaters" (her supervisors) are fuzzy themselves. Now we have all kinds of interference. And it works both ways.

Employees often form their own expectations about the organization, particularly when expectations have not been established. Sometimes, these expectations have little to do with what the leaders of the organization actually say. Employees talk to colleagues, read the business or tech press, observe internal policies, hear rumors, listen to what customers say, and engage in wishful thinking. Each source of interference has the potential to widen the Expectation Gap. When Susan started with the company, the Expectation Gap was easy to bridge, partly because she hadn't formed a lot of expectations and partly because those that might have existed were quickly clarified. However, as time passes, the gap between Susan's expectations and the intent of the organization gets muddled.

Susan isn't alone. In fact, according to our research, her case is more the rule today than the exception. As we reviewed the results of surveys from over 300,000 employees across the globe, we were particularly interested in questions relating to how Expectation Gaps are formed. One theme stood out clearly as a sure-fire gap builder: poor communication.

In the absence of clearly communicated expectations (think two-way radio communication), the Expectation Gap fills with assumptions, misperceptions, and even accusations. Our survey data points this out clearly. Even though company executives feel they are communicating effectively, their words are not making it to the depths of the organization. When we asked these 300,000 workers about organizational communication, 91 percent of senior managers indicated that the level of communication they receive about important issues and expectations was appropriate. However, as the communication flows downhill, 78 percent of mid-level managers responded they had the information they needed to be successful, and just 68 percent of line-level employees responded the same way. Think about what this means to the end result. One-third of all your line-level employees—those closest to your customers—aren't hearing what you're saying.

FIGURE 2.3 Fuzzy Signal, Fuzzy Reception

As the distance between leaders and employees grows, communication gets less clear, and the gap widens. It becomes easy to hear one thing and believe another—or miss a broadcast altogether. And that's just top-down communication. Add in the fact that we haven't yet taken into account the other side's (Susan's) expectations, and that gap gets filled even more with turbulence and distortion. Our database suggests that fewer than half of employees in many of the organizations surveyed feel they have input into important decisions that affect them personally. It's no wonder Susan isn't clear on what to expect. It also means the company isn't hearing what Susan needs to tell them about your product—or your customers' needs and concerns.

The story continues. Our new recruit came out of her onboarding process expecting to receive no bonus in her first year, per company policy. Fine. But since then, she's seen other first-year employees get bonuses for special achievements. She's getting mixed signals. Even the guy in the next cubicle who just watches YouTube videos and picks his nose most of the day got a bonus last week.

Justified or not, Susan has come to expect that her work puts her in bonus territory, particularly when she evaluates her contributions against the contributions of those around her. Besides, she just bought a used Volkswagen, is having problems with the emissions system, and could really put a bonus to good use. Her needs (and her expectations) have changed. Her supervisors aren't aware of these changing expectations, so nobody acts to counter them. Susan now expects a bonus—in her mind, she *deserves* it.

Whether this expectation is logical or not doesn't matter; Susan's expectations and the emotions they provoke will impact her feelings about the company and her superiors, her level of engagement, and her performance. Expectations are now misaligned, and the Expectation Gap may be a canyon that nothing can bridge.

INTERFERENCE AND DISTORTION

The Expectation Gap isn't just about the distance between what employers say and what employees believe, and it's not just about pay and performance. It's also about clear communication and whether that communication is subject to interference and distortion—how much

EGGHEAD ALERT!

Equity Theory

Equity theory is about perceived justice and fairness. It suggests that employees evaluate the equity between their inputs (the work they do) and the outcomes they receive for that work (their reward) against the perceived inputs and outcomes of others. In other words, an employee will make a comparison by looking at her contributions and what she receives in return, and weigh that ratio against what she perceives to be the contributions and returns of her coworkers. When she finds those relationships to be unequal (e.g., when she perceives that she is working harder than a coworker for less pay), she may become distressed and demotivated.

When this occurs, the theory suggests that employees will seek to restore equity by changing the inputs or outcomes in their own minds (their beliefs), altering the actual inputs and/or outputs (working less or demanding more money), or removing themselves from the perceived equity (leaving the organization).[5]

the signal changes over time from its original source to its final listener. Because if management is thinking this. . .

"We've been clear that this next round of funding could be tricky and if we don't get the funds, there are going to be layoffs."

. . . and employees are thinking this . . .

"Companies like ours are getting billion-dollar valuations, so when this next funding round comes through, we're all going to be rich!"

. . . there are going to be some uncomfortable conversations in the break room.

What makes this particular wicket even stickier is that employers can't assume a clear causal relationship between what they do to establish expectations about things like pay, benefits, and time off and how employee expectations evolve. Employee expectations are organic, with a life of their own.

When messages from both parties cross the gap with little interference, things generally run pretty smoothly. Even if some of the information is negative—impending layoffs, for instance—everybody feels that their managers have been straight with them and communicated openly and transparently. Trust grows because employees feel leveled with, heard, and respected. They feel that they can reliably predict the future, so they're willing to invest themselves in becoming fully engaged.

But that doesn't always happen. Just as atmospheric conditions, terrain, and other factors can interfere with radio signals, factors like politics, culture, ego, personal needs, perceived individual contribution, economic realities, and personality conflicts interfere with employees receiving accurate, timely information. In many organizations, leaders simply don't communicate with their people. When they do, actions aren't consistent with stated values. Management sends mixed messages about revenues, compensation, performance expectations, perks, or a thousand other things.

To make matters worse, many managers aren't tuned into the day-to-day realities of the organization, which makes it impossible for them to get ahead of the expectations growing in the soil of their culture. Are they realistic? Irrational? Potentially harmful? Who knows? In this case, ignorance is *not* bliss.

THERE'S ALWAYS A GAP

When signals become distorted between transmitter and receivers, expectations become misaligned and wind up violated. Morale, commitment, and engagement suffer. But even transparent, tight-knit organizations have Expectation Gaps. Even yours.

Don't feel bad; such gaps are fundamental parts of organizational relationships—laws of *human* nature, if you will. Even in the most open, communicative, values-driven company, community, school, or hospital, there will always be a gap between what was actually promised and what people think they've been promised. A leader's job is to be aware of the gap, understand it, manage it, and minimize any damage to engagement, culture, or brand.

> There will always be a gap. Our challenge is to be aware of it, understand it, manage it, and minimize any damage.

EXPECTATION GAPS MATTER . . . A LOT

Whenever our team of researchers analyze levels of engagement in organizations throughout the world, we find the results intriguing. A number of individuals participating in our employee engagement surveys work in what many would consider some of the most difficult or unpleasant conditions possible. Some work more than seventy-five hours per week for years. Some work with prisoners who do all they can to intimidate, threaten, and harass. Others volunteer in locations where poverty, disease, crime, and extreme living conditions are the norm. Some spend months at a time on oil rigs in the middle of the ocean, doing backbreaking work for twelve-plus hours per day in extreme temperatures, seven days a week. Yet they are highly engaged in their work—and they love what they do!

On the other side, we see organizations where employees work forty hours or less each week, have unlimited paid time off, take months of parental leave to tend to family, drop off their pets and laundry at the company reception desk, and eat two gourmet meals per day in the company-sponsored cafeteria. Sure, cushy gig, but they somehow complain continually and are utterly disengaged.

Why the difference? Some of it, obviously, depends on the nature of the employee (insert your favorite Millennials' gripe here). However, as we culled through the responses in our database, a factor stood out: a profound gap in expectations. Those who were disengaged complained about unmet expectations (even though some of these expectations were rather unreasonable). They expected something that simply wasn't there and, either consciously or unconsciously, they disengaged. Those who found engagement in their work typically got exactly what they expected from the job and, consequently, were fulfilled. They got what they signed up for.

We recently worked with a large company that was experiencing an attrition rate of nearly 50 percent, which meant it would, statistically speaking, lose about half of its workforce of 10,000+ employees every year. That's a scary (and costly) figure that caught more than just the attention of the human resources department.

We were asked to conduct follow-up interviews and surveys with those employees who had left. In all, we looked at 4,544 employees across twenty-nine countries. A few of our findings pointed to glaring problems within the company, while some of the results were somewhat confusing at first glance.

First, there didn't appear to be significant turnover during the first six months of employment. Employees were generally content with their jobs. The problem occurred at about the nine-month mark, at which point the number of employees looking to exit went through the roof.

Why then? As we analyzed the results, it became clear. During the first six months, employees were in the honeymoon period. They were learning, trying to figure out their jobs, and being formally trained and mentored, not to mention the fact that they were just grateful to be working for their dream company. It was basically what they had expected from the job—or they simply hadn't yet formed any clear expectations. But something happened between months seven and nine that caused many employees to rethink their employment decision: They began to see that the job they *thought* they had signed on to do was not the job they were actually doing (or would do in the future).

About half of the employees who left during that six- to nine-month time period said that the biggest reason they left was because the job wasn't meeting their expectations. Now, they didn't always come out and express it in those words; they used phrases like "I thought I would have been promoted by now," or "I wasn't given the hours I thought I would," and even "If I had known this is what I'd be doing every day, I wouldn't have taken the job." Moreover, nearly half of these employees stated that their supervisors had never reviewed the expectations of the job with them, and only 40 percent felt the training they received met their expectations. That's a big Expectation Gap. No wonder the company couldn't retain good people. By the way, customer service and quality indicators tanked as well.

DEAR, DID YOU FORGET TO TAKE OUT THE TRASH AGAIN?

As any couple could tell you, Expectation Gaps don't exist just in businesses. Researchers at Ohio State University conducted studies funded by the National Institute of Mental Health to understand this fact. Their studies involved eighty-two couples within the first few months of their first marriages. Researchers videotaped these pairs as they discussed difficult problems confronting their relationships. They also conducted eight tests at six-month intervals for four years, including examining these couples' relationship skills. Of particular interest was whether expectations for marriage happiness (high or low), as well as preconceived expectations as to how spouses should behave, played any role in the overall levels of marital bliss.

Of the eighty-two couples, seventeen were divorced by the end of the study. Of the remaining sixty-five couples, results showed that those who had high expectations for happiness in the early stages of marriage, but poor relationship skills, experienced sharp declines in marital satisfaction over the first four years of marriage. No real aha moment there. But, surprisingly, those with low expectations and low skills didn't show equivalent declines in satisfaction.

Did you catch that? Those who entered the relationship with (a) high expectations and (b) a limited ability to fix bad relationships were in for a bumpy ride. But those with lower expectations (for the relationship and their partner's behavior) and poor relationship skills in areas such as communication didn't experience much of a drop in satisfaction.

Should we lower our expectations for our spouses and forget about developing any relationship skills? Not quite. In fact, as we learned from our earlier Jennings School District example, lowering expectations is *not* the answer. However, according to the researchers, our level of satisfaction depends less on the external conditions of the marriage than it does on whether expectations are met. As they state in their findings: "Satisfaction goes down when a spouse's expectations don't fit with reality."[6] But, then, most couples could have told you that.

This finding is astonishing: Satisfaction within a relationship has less to do with external conditions such as money, leisure time, or compatibility than whether expectations, big and small, are met.

This observation is at the heart of building a transformational Employee Experience (EX). This also explains why those organizations that sink millions of dollars (or yen, or euros) into perks intended to engage their employees are wasting their money. If all along the employee is thinking "This isn't what I signed up for," a few stale doughnuts and a break room Ping Pong table aren't going to fix that. Yet it's clear why firefighters will put their lives on the line every day for strangers, proudly and with passion. It's part of the job they wanted and *expected.*

Engagement, satisfaction, and happiness often depend less on the conditions in which one works and more on whether expectations are aligned and met.

YOUR COMPANY DOESN'T EXIST. YOUR PEOPLE DO.

Although most of us realize that Expectation Gaps exist, they are difficult to identify and diagnose, particularly in a business context. We operate under the illusion that organizations are something more than a group of people working toward a common goal. When you see your business as a network of people, it is much easier to comprehend the myriad complex relationships that are at play within any organization, group, or community.

The trouble with leaders in many organizations is that they view the company as "The Company," an autonomous entity that doesn't need to be understood or afforded respect. In this worldview, employees are replaceable parts, and we don't worry about the feelings of replaceable parts. But here's the thing:

Your company doesn't actually exist.

People, not legal entities on paper, get stuff done. Who makes sales, does the hiring, takes care of the customer, buys the media, teaches the student, or takes out the trash? Does the corporation do that? We cling to the delusion that corporations can take action, make decisions, and even have personalities. But that's a convenient falsehood.

Perhaps the most famous company in history is the Dutch East India Company, chartered in 1602. It is largely recognized as the first company to issue stock to its owners (Wall Street sends its regards), and it was the first multinational corporation in the world. The Dutch government granted it a monopoly on the spice trade.

Since this was the heyday of mercantilism, the Dutch East India Company had quasi-governmental rights, which made it an extremely powerful organization. It had the ability to wage war, imprison convicts, mint its own coins, and establish colonies. Eventually, the company went bankrupt, and its possessions were distributed in 1799. Yet so influential was this organization that its impact on corporate culture, legal structure, and the way we view power in organizations persists to this day.

It's tempting to think of the Dutch East India Company as a living entity in and of itself. In reality, however, the Dutch East India Company was a *legal fiction*, an actual legal doctrine wherein courts assume a fact in order to answer certain questions or solve analytical problems. For example, since a corporation begins its life as a piece of paper, can it really be said that a corporation is capable of entering into contracts or that it has the ability to sue or be sued? Can a corporation ever engage in criminal activities if it doesn't physically exist as a person? Is a corporation capable of a relationship? If you prick it, does it bleed?

It might be tempting to think of Apple (a modern-day version of the Dutch East India Company) and Google as independent cosmic forces. They aren't. Apple achieved greatness not because it existed in and of itself but because of its talented and innovative people. Even with Amazon's amazing logistics systems, it's still the company's people who run this efficient machine. If you want to improve your company's overall success and the way your company treats your customers, look first at your people. That's the real stuff from which great companies are made.

Your organization is your people. Always has been, always will be. If you want performance, loyalty, low turnover, and a legitimate passion for excellence among your workforce, you can't approach communication or relationships as though you're dealing with an organization, because you're not. You're dealing with individuals with differing desires, backgrounds, dreams, expectations, and levels of understanding, brought together for a common purpose. When you understand this fundamental, key fact, you will start to see the nature of your Expectation Gaps, so you can start working on ways to promote alignment. When you view your organization not as a legal construct but as a network of people and relationships, it's easier to see why managing expectations and building strong relationships matters so much.

> Your company doesn't really exist. It's a name-branded intellectual exercise. Your company is your people. Always has been, always will be.

THE KANSAS CITY WAY

The old-fashioned transactional contract—"You come to work and I pay you"—that employers have slid across the table to employees for decades simply doesn't cut it anymore. The old-school "employees should just be grateful to have jobs at all" mentality doesn't work today. Remember, employees have choices. If you want to keep great people, create an environment in which they can choose to be engaged and turn that engagement into a profitable Customer Experience (CX). You've got to look past pay and perks to their hearts, spirits, minds, and hands.

Employers try to do this in all sorts of ways, most of them wrong. Some focus on compensation, benefits, vacation, perks like in-office gyms, and even paid sabbaticals. There's generally nothing wrong with giving your employees those things. Some are needed to establish a base level of compensation (and they're pretty cool). They're useful . . . except that they usually don't work when it comes to creating a great EX. The goal is to cultivate engagement, and engagement doesn't come from splashy office art or departmental paintball excursions. An emphasis on perks is the essence of "digging in the wrong place."

Gaining alignment and understanding, and managing the Expectation Gap, is all about developing mutual respect, trust, and understanding in your organization, because that's what leads to real, deep engagement. People won't engage because you tell them they should, and they won't embrace initiatives to foster Meaning, Autonomy, Growth, Impact, and Connection—MAGIC—in a vacuum. Managing and aligning expectations creates the soil in which engagement can grow.

For a case study, look no further than the 2015 World Champion Kansas City Royals, a small-market baseball club that spent decades as a laughingstock. But when General Manager Dayton Moore came on board in 2007, the organization established a new set of organizational expectations with its players—a new "Contract" for the Royals.

Under this new, aligned approach, the team would stick with players as they developed and struggled, encouraging them to come up through the minor leagues together and forging that impossible-to-manufacture "band of brothers" bond. The Royals followed through, sticking with Mike Moustakas, Salvador Perez, Alex Gordon, and Eric Hosmer through their slumps and down times instead of becoming impatient and giving up on them, as some angry fans and media members encouraged them to do.

When those players hit their stride at the same time in 2014, they had something more than talent; they had a thick-and-thin sense of family that they used to lift each other up and become the greatest comeback team in the history of postseason baseball—first in their 2014 World Series loss to the San Francisco Giants and then in their 2015 win over the New York Mets. The players' genuine care and love for one another also rubbed off on the fans, who set home attendance records as the Royals cruised to a stirring, come-from-behind five-game World Series victory.

If you saw photos of the sea of 300,000 fans who attended the team's victory parade, you saw the evidence. The Royals organization created a stellar Employee Experience, leading to a customer brand with which Kansas Citians have fallen head over heels in love.

IT'S YOUR RESPONSIBILITY

We have found, through both research and our own (often sad) experience, that Expectation Gaps are often at the core of employee disengagement and discontent. As we coach individuals, we frequently find that it's not a lack of desire that holds them back from stellar performance. It's also not lack of skills that keeps them from engaging. It's the Expectation Gap. They simply don't know what's expected, or their expectations differed from those of their supervisors. It's hard to hit a target you didn't know existed.

Right now you might be thinking "it seems like this puts all the responsibility on managers—all on me? What about the times employees misinterpret management's expectations or believe they're entitled to something nutty? Where's their responsibility in all this?"

Fair questions. Often, employees are the problem, like when they cling to unrealistic expectations or misread a company's actions out of cynicism or self-interest. We *will* talk about the employees' role in all this. However, since management's paying the bills (and getting paid by the customer), the onus is on you to have your finger on the pulse of what employees and customers feel and believe.

If you and your employees have a meeting of the minds, alignment of what both sides expect occurs, and everyone feels that promises are being kept and respect given, you'll have an EX that results in fully engaged employees who will also deliver a brilliant CX.

It begins with expectations—bridging that Expectation Gap and then creating Expectation Alignment. That's next.

CHAPTER 2. THE EXPECTATION GAP: THE CHAPTER EXPERIENCE

- Expectations are tools for clarifying the present and predicting the future.
- The environment of expectations within an organization is like a radio transmitter sending a signal to hundreds or thousands of receivers. The clearer the signal, the better the experience.
- The Expectation Gap is the space between sender and receiver where interference can distort the message.
- Expectation Gaps are always present. The degree to which these gaps are affected by distortion and interference defines the success of the relationship.
- Perks don't create sustainable motivation.
- When expectations are not clear, disengagement results.
- Corporations are necessary legal fictions. They aren't real; your people are. People take action, make decisions, and serve customers.
- Engagement depends less on the conditions in which one works than on whether expectations are met.

CHAPTER 3

Ask Your Doctor about Expectation Alignment Dysfunction

> You walk out of a conference room and you'll see a grown man covering his face. Nearly every person I worked with, I saw cry at their desk.
>
> —FORMER AMAZON EMPLOYEE, AS QUOTED BY THE *NEW YORK TIMES*[1]

Based on this quote, you might assume that we find ecommerce behemoth Amazon.com to be a cesspit of tyrannical bosses and downtrodden employees. Not so. We actually want to call your attention to the fact that, though it may seem counterintuitive, Seattle's non-coffee flagship corporation is one of the best in the world at building an aligned, engaged workforce.

Confused? Let us explain.

First, return with us to the thrilling days of yesteryear—to be exact, August 15, 2015, when the *New York Times* ran a bombshell feature that brought the polarizing story of Amazon's internal environment to the public.[1] In it, two reporters paint a grotesque portrait of a corporate Hunger Games in which employees are pushed to (and often beyond) their limits, encouraged to sabotage each other, and, in more than one reported case, treated with stunning indifference in the wake of devastating life events and illnesses.

The result is a workplace guided by what one ex-employee called "purposeful Darwinism," where the weak or ill-suited are weeded out by the simple, merciless Amazon imperative: *Become more excellent every day or perish.* But at what cost? The *Times* story makes some of that cost clear, citing examples of employees being put on performance notice after being out of the office with cancer, others having been given performance improvement plans after recovering from serious illnesses, and still others who were written up after absences for miscarrying or having stillborn children.

Uncaring? Certainly. Ugly? Understatement. Yet Amazon pushed back, insisting that its relentless drive for innovation and customer delight means that its workforce must strive for constant improvement, too. CEO Jeff Bezos got into the act with a letter sent to shareholders in April 2016, in which he defended the company's culture:

> "Someone energized by competitive zeal may select and be happy in one culture, while someone who loves to pioneer and invent may choose another," he said, adding ". . . we've collected a large group of like-minded people. Folks who find our approach energizing and meaningful."[2]

Still, while the beauty of a company's culture may be in the eye of the beholder, there is little doubt that stories like this paint a chilling picture of cold, callous corporate masters who not only don't earn the trust and loyalty of their people but don't even deserve that trust.

However, not everyone views Amazon that way. Some current and former employees have even gone public with their own praise for the company, saying that they appreciate how the high-pressure, perform-or-die culture helped them become smarter and stronger. But what's really interesting is that while Amazon may be a bruising, unforgiving place to work, when you look at the metric of employee satisfaction, the company wins startlingly high marks across the board.

This culture didn't evolve on its own. It was intentionally created when Amazon began its operations. In fact, in a 1997 letter to stockholders, Bezos clearly points this out: "It's not easy to work here (when I interview people I tell them 'you can work long, hard, or smart, but at Amazon.com you can't choose two out of three')." He further adds that employees at Amazon are "working to build something important, something that matters to our customers, something that we can all tell our grandchildren about."[3] Amazon isn't right for every job seeker. The company experiences high turnover. However, it also boasts a steady stream of potential employees knocking at the door. And for those who value quality delivery, exactness, superior customer focus, and best-in-class logistics excellence, while simultaneously adding a few well-respected bullets to a résumé, Amazon may be the place to thrive.

Amazon knows what it is, and attracts, retains, develops, and rewards those who embrace that type of environment.

According to researchers at the University of Kansas, who surveyed 993 companies across all sectors (using data gathered from Glassdoor.com), Amazon ranked sixty-third in overall employee satisfaction.[4] What's strange is that during that same time period, Amazon scored much lower in the area of work-life balance. How do we reconcile a workplace where managers drive their people like Russian Olympic gymnastics coaches with the intense employee loyalty—even love—that we find there? Two words:

Expectation Alignment (EA).

Remember, it isn't so much whether the conditions are good or bad; rather, it's more important that expectations are aligned and reasonably being met. Amazon seems to understand this principle.

WHAT IS EXPECTATION ALIGNMENT?

In more precise language,

> EA is the level to which employees' expectations for their experience in the workplace line up with their *perceived, actual* experiences.

Without EA, a transformational EX cannot be built.

Although Amazon's optics in the media aren't the best, the company excels at EA because it lets new hires know exactly what to expect from their employment and then fulfills those expectations. That doesn't make the company a good fit for everyone, though:

- You're a family man or woman who wants your job to fit into your need for home time, leisure, and rejuvenation: **BAD FIT.**
- You're a Millennial starting your career who's okay with a few years of being work-obsessed, having a limited personal life, and being pushed harder than ever before while building a résumé and being well compensated: **GOOD FIT.**

People who want their workplace to be a love fest filled with Nerf gun fights and interdepartmental yoga are better off sending their résumés to

HubSpot. Ferociously competitive men and women with thick skins and the ability to excel in the clutch, however, often consider Amazon the best place they've ever worked, the employer that helped them hone a world-class skill set. Same environment, different expectations, different outcome.

Employee expectations are the linchpin of the Employee Experience (EX), and they are the result of many factors. Some of the most influential are the explicit promises made to employees during recruiting, hiring, onboarding, and ongoing employment. These include clear expectations around compensation, hours, performance, and other express agreements. But formation of expectations doesn't end there; expectations (implied and express) are constantly being formed throughout the employee life cycle, including:

- **Implied promises from the work environment and company culture.** The everyday environment of an organization implies all sorts of promises. Perhaps a new sales account executive has heard that top sales reps go on international business trips to China and Australia. If he surpasses his sales goals, he may have an expectation of such travel, and if travel budgets have been slashed, he may feel cheated and resentful.
- **Rumors and stories from colleagues and peers.** Rumors and gossip are the enemies of EA because they fill employees' heads with unsupportable claims. Perhaps one of the most common and dangerous is the "they're going to lay people off" rumor, which can lead to everything from panic to workplace sabotage. On the other side of the coin, there is the "management is talking to a venture capital firm and we're all going to be rich!" rumor. Both types can be damaging, and employee behavior will reflect their beliefs about the future state.
- **News stories and other information from the broader culture.** It's not realistic to expect employees to see news coverage of IPOs, unemployment rates, and other business events and not have that information affect what they expect from the future. Expectations are often formed by those outside the organization and transferred to employees.
- **Employer brand.** Your organization has two brands: one with its customers *and* one with current, future, and past employees—your *employer brand.* Your employer brand comes with a host of expectations that will be picked up and carried by your employees, even if some of it is the stuff of urban legend.

- **Unexpressed or unclear employer expectations**. Do your employees know what you expect of them? Are your expectations realistic? Results from our employee survey and 360-degree feedback databases tell us that nearly half of line-level employees feel the boss's expectations are often muddy, or at least not clearly spelled out.[5]

Leaders who want a fully engaged workforce should be constantly aware of facts, opinions, rumors, and emotions flowing in and out of the organization. More important, they should be communicating with employees regularly and clearly about both erroneous expectations and what they *should* expect. But whether it's because they don't understand the need or are too busy, most leaders haven't been doing either.

DecisionWise's surveys over the past ten years reveal that employers consistently fail to understand some critical realities about their people and may be more disconnected from expectations than they believe. For instance, many managers operate under the understanding that money is employees' main motivator. Untrue. Yet they blame employer turnover on the notion that "They got 5 percent more down the street, so they left." Many believe that bonuses and perks do more to impact engagement than simple gestures of recognition. Wrong. Other managers also believe that employees want a hands-off boss, when our research clearly indicates many employees, especially newer ones, crave an available mentor and leader. In other words, managers often seriously misapprehend what their people really want from their Employee Experience (EX).

THE PROBLEM WITH UNKNOWN EXPECTATIONS

A number of years ago, we met with a company that had just been fired by its largest customer. This large software fulfillment firm (we'll call it "Fulfillment Plus") had worked with its customer, one of the world's largest software development firms (we'll call them Behemoth Software), for the previous eight years. In a move that Fulfillment saw as "out of the blue," Behemoth took its business elsewhere, along with 35 percent of Fulfillment's revenue. When the two CEOs got together for a phone conversation, the fulfillment firm learned that Behemoth's reason for leaving was "unmet expectations."

Needless to say, when Fulfillment's CEO met with his senior staff to discuss the loss of a significant chunk of the firm's revenue, he was distraught, and was visibly angry. The executive team sat down for the better part of two days to review performance over the previous year in great detail.

"Did we have quality issues?" "Did we miss any delivery dates?" "Were there any disagreements or personnel issues between the two organizations?" These questions, and others, were all discussed in great detail. The team even went as far as to verify that key Behemoth executives had been sent small gifts during the holidays. Check. They had. In the end, the executives left without clear answers, although they had clear data as to their performance.

Fulfillment Plus requested a final meeting with Behemoth Software, which was immediately granted. Fulfillment came to the meeting prepared with reams of data showing it had delivered on exactly what was asked for. Behemoth then said something that floored the fired vendor: "You delivered on everything we asked for, and we have no complaints. But we had some unmet, unspoken expectations that you haven't met for the past several years. That's the reason we switched vendors."

Unmet, *unspoken* expectations. That's tough to hear, especially if that's the reason you're going to be surviving without one-third of your revenue. But it was too late. Agreements had been signed with other firms, and Fulfillment soon found it difficult to survive. Eventually, the company ended up folding. Curiously, over the next two years, Behemoth also experienced a significant loss on those product lines Fulfillment had previously handled, due largely to quality issues related to switching to the new provider.

It's not that Fulfillment missed expectations per se. It's that the expectations simply didn't exist, at least as far as the vendor was aware. It's hard to meet expectations when you don't know what they are. Yet, that's exactly how many organizations and managers behave—as if their employees do not have any expectations. We can assure you that they do. These organizations move along without a care, thinking that employees will figure it out. Some managers claim they are "empowering their employees to exercise autonomy" by not setting clear boundaries or expectations. In reality, they are simply setting employees up to fail.

As we study managers who have derailing behaviors, we find that one of the most prevalent and damaging is the failure to set clear expectations. In the course of our research, we monitored approximately 480 managers in a large technology firm over a period of three years. The purpose was to identify common behaviors among those managers who had teams that performed well as opposed to those teams that weren't meeting standards.

We weren't surprised by the results. They clearly showed that managers who had teams of engaged people were far more likely to deliver stellar performance than those who didn't. These results are what we expected (in fact, we wrote our last book about that very topic). However, when we broke them down, it was interesting to see one of the key reasons strong teams were engaged was because they had clear expectations. In fact, the need for clear expectations outweighed factors like compensation, working conditions, perks, training, and all other areas. The results were unequivocal: Teams performed well when performance expectations were clear.

The only other area that even came close to the need for clear expectations was recognition. Interesting, as it's hard to recognize and reward for good performance if you don't know whether targets have been hit. (Hint: Recognition and expectations go hand in hand.) This principle is so basic yet so misunderstood (or at least not practiced): Stellar performance without clear expectations is like hoping to hit a target without knowing what that target is, and doing it blindfolded.

The Expectation Gap is the most significant source of employee performance problems organizations face today. Many employees simply don't know what's expected of them. And by the way, managers: Remember that just because you think expectations are clear doesn't necessarily mean that they are clear to employees, or that expectations are aligned.

THE LONG LUNCH

In 2016, *The Guardian* released a story titled "Long Lunch: Spanish civil servant skips work for years without anyone noticing." The article began with the following paragraph:

> Only when Joaquín García, a Spanish civil servant, was due to collect an award for two decades of loyal and dedicated service did anyone realise that he had not, in fact, shown up to work for at least six years—and possibly as many as 14.[6]

Garcia, an engineer, was hired to supervise a waste water treatment plant in Cádiz, Spain. He was given a post on the municipal water board in 1996. It wasn't until 2010, when Garcia was to receive an award for his long service, that the deputy mayor who had originally hired him wondered where the man had gone. Upon quizzing others, including the former manager of the water board, the deputy mayor found that nobody had seen Garcia for several years. When he called Garcia in to ask what he had accomplished over the previous month, the employee could not answer.

A court fined Garcia €27,000, the equivalent of one year's salary. It found that Garcia "had not occupied his office for at least six years" and that he "had done absolutely no work between 2007 and 2010, the year before he retired." But the fine did not extend to previous years of compensation, possibly because some of the responsibility fell to the city, which had failed to lay out expectations and monitor performance.

Garcia admitted to the court that he "may not have kept regular business hours," but he said that he had shown up at the office from time to time. The tribunal concluded that the water board had assumed Garcia was working under the direction of the city council, while the council believed Garcia was answering to the water board.

The Guardian went on to report that Garcia had "made the most of the confusion, becoming an avid reader of philosophy" and an expert in the works of Dutch philosopher Spinoza.[6] Nice. How do we get that gig?

Nature abhors a vacuum. Consider this thought:

> In the absence of clearly defined expectations, we find or create expectations to fill the void.

THE NEW METRIC FOR ORGANIZATIONAL HEALTH

A healthy, positive EX begins with EA. It is the end point of a fairly predictable process:

EXPECTATION ALIGNMENT (EA)

is a key ingredient in . . .

EMPLOYEE ENGAGEMENT (EE)

which helps build and support . . .

a TRANSFORMATIONAL EMPLOYEE EXPERIENCE (EX).

Everything starts with clear expectations. However, those expectations must also be clearly aligned. EA is a critical inflection point for organizations seeking deeper engagement and an EX that delivers customer delight and five-star reviews. When expectations are being fulfilled by employers and employees, you can be confident that communication is open and honest, authenticity is high, and people are engaged. Because EA is where engagement begins and because it forms the basis for a strong EX, EA is one of the most important tools we have found for guiding an organization's trajectory. When employees don't know what to expect, they don't know how to excel.

Aligning expectations is also becoming critical as the workforce changes. The "Gen Y and Gen Z Global Workplace Expectations Study" by Millennial Branding found that while Generation Y (ages twenty-one to thirty-two) and Generation Z (ages sixteen to twenty) workers have a lot in common, they differ in some important ways. For instance, 28 percent of Gen Z workers said money would motivate them to work harder and stay with their employers longer, compared with 42 percent of Gen Y workers.[7] That gap will likely narrow as Gen Zers age and start families, but in the meantime, it's an important difference. In this case, organizational leaders who don't understand the expectations of their younger workers might lose them by prioritizing money over meaning.

EA is fundamental to employer-employee relationships and, thus, fundamental to every facet of a successful organization. However, be careful not to "manage" expectations. That's uncomfortably close to manipulating them. Managing expectations is different than aligning expectations; management implies coercion, while alignment involves agreement and setting clear direction up front.

Aligning expectations is the result of a straightforward process: define, align, measure, hold accountable, and deliver. When we fail to do so, we end up with expectation gaps, poor performance, disagreements, disengagement, and lawsuits.

ZAPPOS'S FAILED EXPERIMENT?

Amazon might be a star at EA, but beloved online shoe and apparel brand Zappos might be a classic case of expectation misalignment. Founded in 1999, the company reached $1 billion in sales by 2008 and was acquired

EGGHEAD ALERT!

Potemkin Village

Although some historians debate the accuracy of the account, the original story of the Potemkin Village has become an analogy to convey the idea that something is better than it really is. According to the story, the governor of Crimea was an admirer of the Russian empress Catherine II. The region had been destroyed by war, and Potemkin had been tasked with rebuilding the area. A new war was about to break out, and the empress set out with a party of foreign ambassadors with hopes of impressing them into uniting with the Russian cause.

In order to impress those accompanying the imperial party, Potemkin erected "mobile villages" along the banks of the river. He instructed his men to dress as peasants and "populate" the villages as the entourage passed, thus giving the appearance of a thriving village. Once the empress's barge departed, the village was disassembled and erected downstream overnight, giving the party the impression that the region was thriving.

Whether the account is exaggerated or not, the term "Potemkin Village" is a fitting analogy for the façade many organizations put up today.

by Amazon in 2009 for $1.2 billion. The future was so bright, CEO Tony Hsieh had to wear shades—until he egregiously violated employee expectations. Despite the common misconception that workers like to be left alone, in survey after survey employees strongly prefer to have superiors who are easily available and proactive. People like leadership and boundaries within which they can exercise a reasonable amount of self-direction; it creates a comfort level. And that's where Zappos comes in.

Hsieh threw that comfort level to the wind when he adopted *holacracy*, a radical management experiment that did away with leadership and hierarchies in the hope of fostering autonomy and collaboration. The move knocked eyebrows into the stratosphere and provoked a great deal of harrumphing, "We'll see" press coverage.

We've seen, and the results have been mixed. Some employees loved holacracy, saying that it helped them get their ideas heard. But many hated it, feeling that the company had descended into chaos with no one in charge. Turnover jumped by 50 percent from 2014 to 2015. Eighteen percent of Zappos employees accepted a severance package because they couldn't see themselves working in a leaderless environment. One called holacracy a "social experiment" that "created chaos and uncertainty." Most revealing, in 2016 Zappos fell off the *Fortune* "Best Companies to Work For" list—a list it had placed on since 2008.[8]

Is holacracy a failure? Maybe. The fallout suggests it is. Employees want more than a self-initiated job description (unless they're working for a city water board in Spain). They want regular follow-up on how they're doing. They want to know about their progress—even their failures. They want feedback so they can do better. Alignment of expectations, and clear feedback as to performance versus expectations, is critical to performance.

Zappos isn't ready to collapse, is learning from its mistakes, and may yet return to its wildly profitable ways. But the lesson is clear: When even the healthiest company, with the best brand and strongest culture, messes with traditional expectations and its core EX, it does so at its peril. When you *increase* the Expectation Gap and decrease EA, you're flirting with disaster.

Expectation Alignment is fundamental to employer-employee relationships and, thus, is fundamental to every facet of a successful organization.

THE SIX EA PILLARS

On one hand, while working conditions at Amazon may have sparked outrage, employees praise the company and we laud its EA. On the other hand, a shift in the warm-fuzzy, close-knit Zappos culture has made it a cautionary tale.

Organizational culture is self-sustaining, like the Hab (the inflatable building the astronaut calls home) in the Matt Damon movie *The Martian*. As long as things proceed predictably inside, it doesn't matter how hard the dust storm is howling outside. Unless someone is breaking the law or behaving unethically, employees typically will soldier on through even the most challenging workloads and environments, provided they have realistic expectations and the employer consistently meets or exceeds those expectations.

What the outside world thinks about how an organization handles employee expectations doesn't matter as much as whether the organization is internally consistent with what we call the Six EA Pillars. These pillars support the bridge over the Expectation Gap and determine your level of Expectation Alignment.

Despite the fact that Amazon acquired Zappos in 2009, the way these companies handle EA is clearly different. Amazon brings consistency to our Six Pillars; Zappos violated several of them with holacracy. That's how an ecommerce darling selling shoes lost nearly a third of its headcount, while a digital Dickensian workhouse can't hire people fast enough.

The Six EA Pillars

1. **Fairness.** Fairness is a commitment to doing what is equitable for the employer and employee, and honoring both the word and spirit of the "contract" they have with each other. Fairness implies that everyone will be treated according to established rules and will be rewarded in a manner proportionate to his or her abilities and performance.
2. **Clarity.** Clarity is built by taking the time to understand the other party's point of view. As Dr. Stephen R. Covey has said, it's about seeking to first understand before seeking to be understood.[9] Clarity means building an agreed-on set of assumptions that form the basis for a deal or a relationship (i.e., the primary assumptions). It's about identifying what both employer and employee hope to get from the relationship and describing those expectations in detail and without any ambiguity. Clarity also requires maintenance. As times and conditions change, both employer and employee must take care to communicate clearly about what's happening from their side of the negotiating table.
3. **Empathy.** Empathy is about seeing the value in others' viewpoints. It's the ability to put oneself in others' shoes and to see and *feel* their emotions as they consider the upside, the risks, and the fears that are part of forming a bargain or a relationship. When both managers and employees take the time to empathize with others, and see one another as real people, the likelihood of EA increases significantly.
4. **Predictability.** Both parties need to approach the relationship in a consistent manner. This doesn't mean either party can't change its mind, but it does mean each owes the other party an explanation when this does occur. It also means that nobody changes the primary assumptions that form the basis of the original agreement unless they intend to unwind or redefine the relationship. Everyone honors the primary

assumptions and recognizes how essential they are to the relationship. Predictability also means approaching workplace situations consistently from day to day and year to year. There are no surprises.

5. **Transparency.** Transparency is about disclosing the motives and reasons behind decisions. It's making sure there are no skeletons in the closet that need to be dealt with. Managers don't hold back from sharing information that might impact employees, and employees are open with matters concerning the organization. In other words, nothing is hidden. Each party is open and candid about anything that, if it were disclosed later, would have a material impact on the relationship.
6. **Accountability.** This is about being responsible for the terms of the relationship and what occurs within each part of it. Accountability means employer and employee, manager and subordintate, own their outcomes according to the terms of the "contract" and don't try to avoid them. It means promises.

As we researched and identified these Pillars, we asked, "Does every one of these Pillars need to be in place in order to have Expectation Alignment within an organization?" After all, even some of the strongest companies we mention in this book appear to be deficient in at least one.

To answer this question, we turned to employee survey results from more than 400 organizations of all sizes and industries across the globe (over 70 countries). The answer? First of all, the more Pillars an organization had in good standing, the better its EA. That makes sense. But our research showed us something we didn't expect: The magic number appears to be four.

We found that when at least four of the Pillars are in place and strong, you have EA. Furthermore, in organizations where at least four Pillars were consistently present, the level of employee engagement was 25 to 30 percent higher, on average, than in those that had fewer than four. Four appears to be a clear cutoff point. Fewer than four Pillars, and EA suffers and the EX degrades. With just one or two, you have misalignment and a distrustful, disengaged workforce.

For all its flaws, Amazon is clear about what employees should expect. Its methods and outcomes are predictable. The company is transparent about its motives: to build the world's most valuable company by finding employees who kick butt under pressure. Everyone appears to be held accountable for their choices. On the downside, feedback channels that employees use to undermine each other mean their Fairness Pillar is weak, and empathy is not Amazon's strong suit. But the company has reinforced the remaining four Pillars it needs to thrive.

ASK YOUR DOCTOR ABOUT EAD

So, are you suffering from what we call Expectation Alignment Dysfunction, or EAD? You can insert your own punchline here about embarrassing medical conditions, but this actually is an unfortunate problem affecting organizations and teams of all types.

Consider the American Institute of Certified Public Accountants. In response to widely publicized corporate ethical issues, the institute embarked on a series of studies to identify auditors' roles in understanding and monitoring the inner workings of the organizations to which they provide service. The group identified one of its biggest challenges as "the difference between what the public . . . believe[s] auditors are responsible for and what auditors themselves believe their responsibilities are."[10]

Sometimes the public—and even company executives—believe that auditors will find everything that's wrong within an organization. The auditors, however, are quick to point out that they have a limited supply of resources and time and limited access to people, information, and facilities. Therefore, they can't possibly be expected to uncover every potential issue. This is a real misalignment that is fraught with potential liability. Think Enron.

Misalignment also shows up with alarming frequency within the walls of an organization. Employers and employees often have a disconnect in expectations, and this misalignment results in poor performance and disengagement. An employee starts setting his own expectations before he even becomes an employee—when he first comes into contact with your brand. (More on this later.) Expectations continue to form during the interview, and then, if he's hired, they go on crystallizing during onboarding *and every day thereafter*. Expectations are aligned when the expectations that an employee forms at a point in time (usually early on in employment) match up with the sum of his perceived interactions over time.

Let's say a new hire (we'll call him Steve, a good, solid name) comes on board at your company. When he's hired, he has four main expectations (some explicit, some implicit) already set in his mind:

1. There are opportunities for advancement in his department.
2. He will not be expected to work on weekends.

3. The company is a fun, easygoing place to work.
4. He will receive a performance review in one year.

After a year, your company has fulfilled those expectations reasonably and fairly. Steve has been able to submit proposals to take on more responsibility, though none has been approved yet. He has not been asked to work weekends. He's gone on several company outings and received a comprehensive performance review. He's satisfied that you've kept your promises, and trust has started to build. Steve's Expectation Gap looks like the one shown in Figure 3.1.

Notice that the path is steady from the beginning of the year to the end, and that all Pillars are in tact. That's EA. Steve's experience as an

FIGURE 3.1 Six Pillars of Expectation Alignment

employee closely matches his expectations at the outset of his employment. His EX is aligned with his expectations. The Six Pillars support his experience, which means he feels he's been treated with clarity, fairness, and so on. He's having a good EX.

Now, suppose things go differently. Steve is pressured to work weekends, the only "employee outing" was a kid's night at a Chuck E. Cheese's knockoff, and his performance review was a quick "keep it up" in the hallway. His gap will look more like the one shown in Figure 3.2:

That's Expectation Misalignment. Steve feels he was lied to. He is resentful toward his boss and the company, and is not having a good

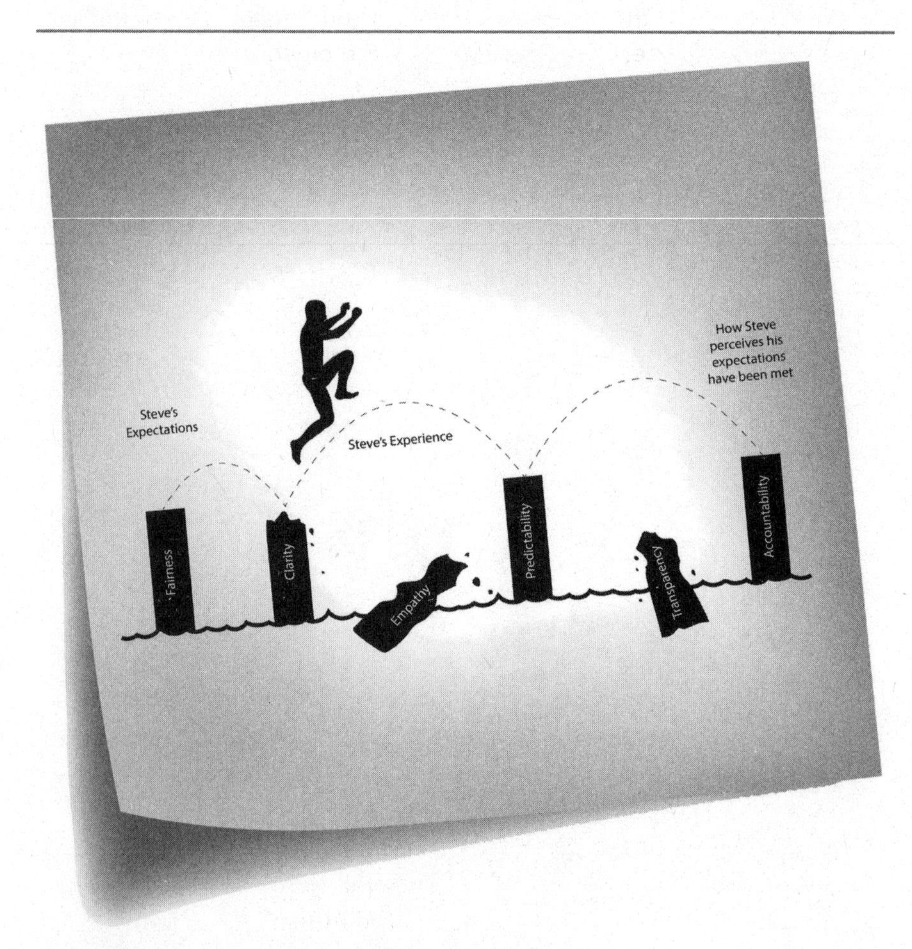

FIGURE 3.2 Expectation Misalignment

experience. Multiply this situation by a few dozen or a few hundred employees, and you have EAD.

EAD occurs when a critical mass of people in an organization or team feel that their expectations for work have not been met. That's a recipe for a terrible EX, disengagement, and failure.

When EAD occurs, it doesn't matter whether employee expectations are reasonable and realistic or not. To your employees, they are. That means whether you agree with those expectations or not, you must account for and deal with them.

> EA occurs when the expectations that an employee forms at a point in time (often from the beginning of employment) match up with the sum of his or her perceived interactions with the organization.

EAD SYMPTOMS AND CAUSES

Diagnosing EAD becomes easier if you know what to look for. Early warning signs of EAD include:

- Lower employee engagement, with no clear cause.
- Increased stress and anxiety levels among workers.
- Increased turnover or talk of resignations.
- Employees not meeting goals or benchmarks.
- Anger and resentment among employees.
- The persistent spread of negative rumors about individuals or the organization.
- Quality issues.
- An increase in customer dissatisfaction.

There are many more symptoms, but the tricky part is spotting them in their early stages before trust, the critical element of engagement, is gone. But here's the problem—when many organizations experience these warning signs, they attack them through operational means. They redesign assembly lines, roll out new products, or even restructure the company to move out the dissenters. They fail to realize that alignment problems cannot be fixed with operational solutions!

The scary thing about EAD is that it's like cardiovascular disease: You can't always go in and fix it after it happens. Just as cardiologists can't always Roto-Rooter dangerous plaques out of clogged coronary arteries, managers can't magically repair trust once it's broken. Most of the time, when trust between employer and employees is gone, it's gone. Stopping EAD is all about *prevention.* Recovery after damage has occurred is a difficult, painful process.

To prevent any disease, you have to know what causes it. Just as there are Six Pillars that breed aligned expectations, there are six factors that make EAD likely, even inevitable:

1. **Lack of clarity.** Opportunities, rules, benefits, quality standards, and other essentials are not made clear at the beginning of employment or throughout an employee's tenure. This can also mean that managers don't tell employees plainly what they expect, making it improbable that employees meet those expectations.
2. **Inconsistency.** Rules and policies are enforced differently based on the circumstances or are enforced differently for some employees than for others.
3. **Overpromising.** Managers set employees up to expect a lot and then can't (don't) deliver, whether intentionally or unintentionally.
4. **Asymmetrical expectations.** Managers expect one thing from employees while employees expect something else, and the two sides never reconcile the differences.
5. **Secrecy.** Managers make too many decisions behind closed doors, leading to . . .
6. **Unchecked rumors.** Employees cultivate rumors about everything from company direction to preferential treatment, and managers don't address them.

Note that we didn't include things like layoffs, down cycles, or other negative events as causes of EAD. That's because those things, *in and of themselves*, need not necessarily breed EAD . . . if employee expectations about them are set realistically and respected. Even a financially healthy company, however, can be brought low if it ignores the EAD warning signs.

Look at the disaster that befell the employees of Lehman Brothers when the venerable bank shockingly filed for bankruptcy back in 2008 at the beginning of the recession. Secrecy was toxic and expectations were completely asymmetrical. Upper management knew that the mortgage bond market was based on fraud, and manipulated accounting records and financial accounts to prevent losses. Meanwhile, the rank and file thought their jobs were secure and Lehman was untouchable.

As Maurice Elvekrog, a management psychologist and chairman of personal money management company Seger-Elvekrog said, "Employees and the public had the expectation, like with the *Titanic*, that you didn't have to worry about these firms."[11]

After Lehman went bust, many of the company's executives and money managers quickly found work at other banks. However, the majority of the company's 25,000 employees, who were not financial wizards but clerical workers and security and operations staff, lost not only their jobs but their stock packages and, in many cases, severance pay. Employees who trusted that their mighty employer would never steer the ship into the rocks ended up as flotsam after the wreck while their superiors took all the lifeboats.

PREVENTING EAD

Like heart disease, EAD is deadly to nearly all organizations. Employees who don't trust the company, or feel betrayed and lied to, become a destructive force, even if they don't intend to be. They deliver terrible customer service because they don't care. They let bad products flow down the assembly line. They fail to drive the desired results. They're more likely to disengage completely, shambling through their daily tasks, doing just enough not to get fired, and infecting others with their ennui and apathy. They can even become saboteurs, consciously or unconsciously.

You can prevent this by first understanding two key concepts. First, EA is not static in time. You can evaluate it from the moment an employee begins employment, but you don't stop there. You can gauge EA from the time an employee starts in a new position, from immediately after a performance review, from the beginning of a pivotal project, or from just about any other point. Through the ups and downs of challenging work, have the employee's expectations been met?

The end point is crucial because of the second key concept. EA isn't about an absolute measurement; it's about the change, also known as the *delta*. Take another look at Steve's EA graphs in Figures 3.1 and 3.2.

Steve starts off as a happy camper, right? But what if Steve's manager takes a look at his EA in a year and finds that a couple of the Pillars are a little shakey? The absolute change is small, but the implications are huge: Expectations are slipping out of alignment, and this great employee's experience isn't as satisfying.

Although there are certainly more, we've listed five effective, proven ways you can inoculate your organization against the dangerous effects of EAD:

1. **Take the temperature.** Find out what employees are thinking and what they expect. Talk to them openly and honestly. Have the conversations that need to take place. You don't have to conduct formal surveys, although they certainly help. Create confidential feedback channels to encourage regular, candid opinions. Keep your finger on your people's pulse. Ask, then listen.
2. **Cross-check expectations.** Connect with individual employees at the department or work group level about what they expect and how those expectations are being met. Let them also know what you're expecting from them, as well as what the organization expects. Open discussions mean that nothing festers behind the scenes. Remember, expectations always exist, whether implicit or explicit. So, get them out in the open.
3. **Do some cultural pruning.** In some organizations, aspects of the internal culture encourage people either to form unrealistic expectations or to have expectations that mutate irrationally. A great example is the Silicon Valley startup world, where talk of stock options leads everybody to think they're going to be millionaires. Cultural pruning minimizes or excises aspects of your culture that encourage harmful expectations.
4. **Use intentional language.** Observe the language the organization uses, as well as that of individual managers, for how it might inflate expectations, overpromise, or provoke fears of secrecy or falsehood. Avoid "corporate-ese." Speak plainly and honestly.
5. **Monitor known expectations.** Ensure that the "right" expectations are reinforced and that "wrong" expectations are minimized.

EAD RECOVERY

In 2015, Goldman Sachs embarked on an initiative to retain its younger investment bankers who, over the previous few years, had been exiting the company after a predictable two-year employment tenure.

The company, recognized for its hard-driving culture, realized that watching its talent and knowledge walk out the door was the painful fallout of EAD.

The banking firm found that its analysts—bright, overachieving, recent college graduates—were joining with the expectation that they would put in their two years and leave with a good deal of applicable knowledge and an impressive set of bullets on their résumés. Those qualifications would then position them for what they considered to be more ideal jobs in the corporate world or other financial firms. As such, the young financial whizzes often viewed themselves as indentured, although willing, servants for two years, generally working seventy-hour workweeks and pulling frequent all-nighters.

The firm, in contrast, had expectations that these up-and-comers would see a career at Goldman Sachs as a long-term investment rather than a short-term warm-up for what they really wanted. After all, the firm offered high salaries and opportunities that would prepare them for future work in the financial industry. Unfortunately, the firm found that while it was succeeding in its objectives in bringing on the best and the brightest, the expectation that this would result in these young analysts sticking around was not met. A clear case of EAD.

During this same time, Wall Street was experiencing a tragic wave of suicides, brought on, in part, by what was attributed to the frantic pace and stress associated with investment banking.[12] Goldman, realizing that the investment banking business is only as good as the people working there, set out to realign and redefine expectations.

First, Goldman began working on eliminating busywork and mundane tasks. The task force recognized that these intelligent new employees expected to use their college learning and drive immediately in their new roles. Instead, they often faced routine tasks that were monotonous, at best. They were bored to tears. So, the company looked to technology to automate these tasks rather than requiring junior personnel to plow through the tedious work.

Second, the firm initiated a 12-month rotation program, so that new employees would gain exposure to other parts of the business. That way, they were able to continue learning while gaining valuable insights into other areas within Goldman that might pique their interests. The firm accelerated promotions after the second year, along with accompanying increases in salaries.

Goldman also created its "junior banker task force." Among its first initiatives was to prohibit analysts from working from 9 p.m. on Friday to 9 a.m. on Sunday; it also set the clear expectation that interns should leave the office before midnight each evening. This eliminated the perception that junior staff were expected to work the all-nighters for which the position had been infamous.[13] Although Goldman employees expected a grueling two years, they hadn't expected the life-consuming realities their new roles involved. The new schedule was intended to send the message that employees were not expected to live a life of servitude.

Did this realignment result in a change in the EX? Goldman has been quiet about its attrition figures. Are Goldman Sachs employees still working long hours in a stressful environment? Probably. It's likely that the firm will always have a highly driven culture, with high expectations. That's in its DNA. However, we suspect that the realignment has made, and will make, a difference. Goldman set out to first listen and understand, then align expectations. When expectations are aligned, great things happen to the EX.

CHAPTER 3. ASK YOUR DOCTOR ABOUT EXPECTATION ALIGNMENT DYSFUNCTION: THE CHAPTER EXPERIENCE

- Poor leaders manage expectations; great leaders align them.
- Expectation Alignment (EA) is a foundational element of the Employee Experience (EX). EA gauges how well an employee's experience matches his or her expectations from one point in time to another. The better the experience matches the expectations, the better the EA.
- EA can be affected by express and implied promises, rumors, employer expectations, and the wider culture.
- Because EA leads directly to a winning EX, it is one of the most important metrics for determining the health of your organization.
- A company can have a strong EA even with a demanding culture because expectations are clearly set and met.
- EA is built on Six Pillars: fairness, clarity, empathy, predictability, transparency, and accountability.
- Expectation Alignment Dysfunction (EAD) occurs when a critical mass of people in an organization or team feel lied to or that what they had expected isn't the reality they experience.
- The factors that most often lead to EAD are lack of clarity, inconsistency, overpromising, asymmetrical expectations, secrecy, and unchecked rumors.
- Effective preventive measures include temperature taking, cross-checking, cultural pruning, intentional language, and expectation reinforcement or minimization (depending on the circumstances).

CHAPTER 4

An Intentional Framework

Is anyone else freaking out right now? I'm kind of freaking out.[1]

—GRAVITY PAYMENTS CEO DAN PRICE,
IMMEDIATELY AFTER ANNOUNCING HIS $70,000 MINIMUM SALARY PLAN

After the last few chapters, it should be abundantly clear that if you want a transformational Employee Experience (EX) that will improve your organization, begin by defining, managing, and aligning expectations. Indeed, everything you write, say, or do from a position of leadership—whether you're an owner, an HR director, a principal, or a team supervisor—impacts employee expectations and the EX. Be mindful of the words you use and the face you show the world. People are paying attention, even if you think they're not.

Gravity Payments CEO Dan Price learned this the hard way. He admits that he wasn't terribly mindful of EX back in late 2011 when an employee took him aside and angrily accused Price of refusing to pay him enough to "lead a decent life." The recrimination sent Price into a tailspin of guilt and soul-searching. He began handing out 20 percent raises, and finally, in April of 2015, he made an Earth-shattering announcement: Gravity Payments would begin phasing in a $70,000 minimum wage over the next three years. Price would cut his own salary from $1.1 million to $70,000 to help pay for it.

The business press went ballistic. Price appeared on the cover of *Inc.* with the headline "Is This the Best Boss in America?" Rush Limbaugh called his action "pure, unadulterated socialism."[2] Harvard Business School asked to study the effects of the raise on the company and its workforce. Overnight, Price went from just another wunderkind tech company CEO to a celebrity. Publicity stunt? Maybe. A bad business decision that will come back to bite both Gravity and Price? We'll see. But it's certainly an interesting case study.

As you would imagine, since the announcement, Gravity has been besieged by job applications. Revenue went up 35 percent in 2015, and profits jumped from $3.5 million to $6.5 million, some of which was probably due to the flood of publicity the company received. The big shift also brought a lot of scrutiny and negative publicity, including an accusation of fraud and a lawsuit from Price's brother. But to us, the most interesting thing about Price's decision was its impact on employee expectations and the employee state of mind.

Many employees reported lower stress and anxiety levels, along with an improved focus on work, which makes sense because they're not worrying as much about making ends meet. *USA Today* reported:

> Employee turnover fell 19% last year compared to the average of the past six years. Gravity has been flooded with 30,000 applications, up from an average 3,000 or so a year. . . . Retirement account contributions are up 130%, more employees are buying first homes.[3]

Price's risky decision obliterated existing employee beliefs and put in place a set of new expectations that appear to have been beneficial. Gravity employees seem to be more invested, and that's obviously good for business.

Although we're not advocating that organizations look to hefty raises to increase the levels of employee engagement within their ranks (in fact, we're against it), Gravity truly is a curious experiment. The question remains as to whether it will pay off in the long run. The evidence is clear: Money is not a long-term motivator. (We hope you've picked that up in the first few chapters!) But Price set a new expectation—one that said "as an employee, you can expect us to watch out for you financially," and it's that resetting of expectations that is likely to play the greatest role in engagement. People who believe that an organization really has their best interests at heart, and does what it says it will do, will walk through fire to make it more successful.

SHAPING BELIEFS

Expectation Alignment (EA) shapes what employees believe. Employee beliefs separate engaged, harmonious organizations from those that seem disengaged or embroiled in costly conflict. Beliefs are the operating system of the mind *and* of this nebulous thing we call an organization. What people believe to be true about themselves, other people, the team, the organization, and the world influences how they feel. They way they feel influences how they think, and how they think determines how they behave (which ultimately impacts the success of the organization).

What do you want your employees to believe about you and your organization? More important, what do they *already* believe? Do they believe that you are looking out for their best interests or that it's company first, people second? Do they believe that you'll keep your promises or discard them as soon as keeping them becomes inconvenient? Do they believe that you mean it when you say "We're a team" or "We're a family" or that it's empty rhetoric without any substance?

Do they believe that you're all in this together for the same purpose and acting according to the same values or that management plays by its own rules and employees are interchangeable parts of an assembly line? Most important of all, are you content to let employee beliefs and expectations form on their own or would you rather shape them intentionally? Again, we're not talking about manipulating what employees think, but emphasizing the facts, philosophies, and qualities around which you hope they will form their beliefs and expectations.

Beliefs and expectations are like nature; they abhor a vacuum. Put a group of people in a demanding environment without any context about the people running the show and they will draw their own conclusions. It's human nature.

The problem is, in the absence of clearly defined expectations, they often draw misleading conclusions that aren't helpful based on evidence they don't fully understand. It's the job of leaders at all levels to provide context, guide their people to fair, fact-based conclusions, and set and meet expectations in such a way that their beliefs help build the organization rather than harm it.

I GET IT, BUT HOW?

We've spent a lot of time presenting a case as to why it's absolutely critical that leaders align and shape expectations. It's been a cautionary tale, and we can feel your fingers starting to dig into the pages as you exclaim in frustration: "I get it! But how can I actually manage the myriad of expectations that exist in a complex organization or team? How do I possibly align every expectation?"

The answer isn't found in a new management theory or in developing certain skills during a workshop. Moreover, the answer doesn't reside in techniques or traits that a leader can develop and nurture. The answer lies in a lot of hard work and by building an intentional plan that focuses on how you will align the expectations for which you are responsible.

Let's consider a success story familiar to many. What was Apple like when Steve Jobs came back to run the company in 1997? It certainly wasn't the world's most valuable company you know today. This version of Apple was clinging to life and coming off a series of product failures; rumor was that Sun Microsystems would buy it. It would have been very easy for Apple employees at the time to panic and run for the exits. But they didn't, and the credit for that goes to Jobs. One former employee (and former CEO of Mozilla), John Lilly, remembered a speech Jobs gave upon his return:

> [Jobs admitted] that the stock price was terrible . . . and that what they were going to do was reissue everyone's options on the low price, but with a new three-year vest. He said: "If you want to make Apple great again, let's get going.[4]

Jobs didn't allow expectations or beliefs that didn't serve Apple's welfare to remain or take root. He spoke plainly and emotionally. He had a plan, and he challenged his people to believe. His plan was intentional and deliberate, setting clear expectations. Given Apple's basically vertical climb since then, it's a safe bet that employees bought into Jobs's vision. And Jobs's second go-round at Apple is an even clearer example of intentionally shaping employee beliefs and expectations so that they serve the organization instead of hinder it.

FIRST, CHALLENGE YOUR INHERITANCE

Our consulting experience has taught us that most organizations inherit their Employee Experiences and leadership styles. Whatever exists was either forged by the founders or built during past administrations. Despite this, most organizations seem to accept those organizational values without question, as if they were divinely appointed.

But does your organization or team really have the right EX to meet its objectives? Was it right from the beginning? Is it right now? Some might call it heresy to ask these types of questions. Steve Jobs didn't. Tony Hsieh with Zappos has shown that he is not afraid to question conventional wisdom. Each man questioned what others might jealously guard as their rightful inheritance. Transformation and innovation can be found only by asking questions and looking for a better way. So, give yourself permission to act like a Millennial and to start questioning your current EX. What is the right EX and leadership style that will best suit your business objectives?

LEADERS ARE THE CUSTODIANS OF THE EMPLOYEE EXPERIENCE

After a period of intense, therapeutic questioning, begin your work at the macro level. Examine your foundational beliefs and core values, whether they be for your organization, division, or team. Looking through the lens of the employee, beneficial beliefs and values might look something like this:

- The organization has my back.
- The leaders are as good as their word.
- It's okay if I take a risk and fail.
- The best people rise to the top here.
- My boss cares about my life away from work.
- It's worth it.

These beliefs and values, however, are not so beneficial:

- The organization doesn't care about me.
- My manager overpromises and underdelivers.
- When it comes to customers, it's all about profitability.
- Only people who are willing to play the game advance around here.
- I can't fail or I'll be fired, so I'd better play it safe.
- If I come up with a great idea, it won't matter anyway.

It's easy to appreciate how the first set of beliefs would empower employees to take risks, be creative, and fully engage while the second would encourage them to do the minimum and fall into cynicism and resentment. Which employees would you rather have on your payroll?

> Your organization's core beliefs and values are its operating system. What people believe to be true influences how they feel. How they feel influences how they think, and how they think determines how they behave.

After carefully considering your foundational beliefs and core values, your next task is to understand the pivotal role the EX plays in the health of any organization. A focus on EX and EA changes the responsibilities of every stakeholder:

- **Entrepreneurs and founders.** The people who launch organizations are in a unique position to establish expectations from the beginning of a business. If you're in that position, it means you have the privilege of intentionally shaping beliefs in a way that strengthens your organization. It also means that if you're not mindful of employee expectations, you can fall prey to the inflated expectations that plague many young companies.
- **Senior executives.** Occupants of the C-suite, who commonly focus on the classic business functions, such as marketing, finance, technology, and operations, must first consider how their organization's current and future EX creates an operating environment that either supports or detracts from its long-term goals. For example, a company's chief operating officer might adapt a company's customer service structure to benefit from the committed support approach of an engaged workforce.
- **Vice presidents and senior managers.** Senior managers usually see things from 30,000 feet. But an EX focus tends to redirect their energies toward keeping their fingers on the pulse of their departments through ongoing conversations, surveys, dashboards, feedback, and communication tools.
- **Managers and supervisors.** Working closely with teams and individuals makes managers the foot soldiers of the EX. Managers and supervisors connect with employees and customers individually and directly, learning about their challenges, desires, fears, and goals. They are the beginning and the end of in-house EX management: the

beginning because much of the organic information about what people feel and believe comes from them; the end because they implement EX practices and policies.

DESIGN THINKING AS A BUSINESS MANAGEMENT TOOL

This approach to creating and managing an organization is an adaptation of the school of thought known as *design thinking.* Conceived by David Kelley, founder of innovative design firm IDEO, design thinking is an approach to business innovation that focuses not on just solving problems but, rather, on creating solutions and getting an organization to ambitious goals. Three elements—people, technology, and business—are applied to create multiple possible solutions to a situation, always with the customer or user at the center. As in traditional design, no idea is too wild, no approach is too innovative, and failure is not only tolerated, but welcomed.

Our approach is to apply design thinking to EX. Instead of orienting all ideas around the customer or on the organization itself, they're focused on the employee, with the thought that if the organization has an extraordinary EX woven into its DNA, an extraordinary Customer Experience (CX) becomes inevitable. According to design thinking, EX is not a stack of independent initiatives; it's an integrated design built into the fabric of the organization. Design thinking goes beyond problem analysis ("How do we fix this?") to transformation ("How do we become something different?"). It's the convergence of art and science.

A well-designed EX is about creating a better future, rather than focusing obsessively on keeping employees from becoming dissatisfied through perks, employee bonuses, and the like—the old model for addressing these issues. It's based on management assumptions that differ completely from the old "employees are just out to collect a paycheck and do as little work as possible" thinking. Rather, it follows a new understanding.

Most employees want to achieve and excel in their work. Human nature is to want to engage in what we do. We want to care, and employees will care about the organization, the team, and the customer if they know the organization cares about its employees. In fact, employees will commit to the organization for reasons other than money. Building your EX through design thinking requires leaders at all levels to begin incorporating this type of thinking into all their initiatives, leadership decisions, and strategies.

DESIGN THINKING IN ACTION

Design thinking is at the heart of Big Ass Fans, the Lexington, Kentucky–based heating and cooling company with a less than politically correct name and a bold way of doing business that's changing an old industry. CEO Carey Smith is executing a "200-year vision" called "cultivating chaos" that not only challenges the status quo but focuses on giving his 1,000+ employees the room to push themselves and be creative. In our conversations with Smith, he clearly points out that the company's success is a result of an employee-centered culture.

"It's not about being contrarian in terms of product development and design, but about the way the processes in the company are organized," he says. "Things are very fluid. We joke that you could go on a vacation for three weeks and come back and you might not have the same job. But we're constantly looking for better ways to service the customer, and oftentimes that means rearranging the way we think about business processes.

"I often tell people that if you came to work here it could be the best place on Earth or it could be a living hell," Smith continues. "Things here constantly change. I don't think it looks chaotic to us on the inside, but that's also because the kind of person we attract is someone who's at home with what others would feel is chaotic. We've had a few people come work for us and it's too much. They're looking for 'Here's my job, it stays within this silo, this is what I can expect,' and it's nothing like that here."[5]

Smith's plans for the company include aggressive overseas expansion, and he expects employees who open up foreign markets to commit to staying overseas for at least two years—a heavy commitment for people with young families. But, he says, the company enjoys tremendous "fit" with the people who do commit to his vision. "We try to be really honest with people who are coming on and explain this to them," he says. "But we also have a really high retention rate, close to 90 percent. We accept fewer people, percentage-wise, than Harvard. Even though we're in the middle of Kentucky, we attract people from both coasts. The other day, we interviewed somebody from Cambridge, and I don't mean Massachusetts."

There's also a refreshing strain of idealism in Smith's vision. "When I got out of school, for some idiotic reason I assumed (as a lot of kids do) that I was going to find a place where I would learn the business, be recognized, and move through the ranks," he says. "That's just not the case. So what we've tried to do here is build it the way you thought companies were run when you got out of school. We're very transparent, and the only things we won't put up with are laziness and dishonesty. This is the way you thought your life was supposed to be: engaged and interested. For some people, that may be difficult, but for the type of people we're looking for, they slide right into it."

BETTER DESIGN THROUGH THREE LENSES

What makes Smith's company unique—and earned it a spot on *Inc.'s* fastest-growing companies list for nine consecutive years as well—is not merely manufacturing and distribution prowess. It's the seamless, aligned culture of commitment to human beings that runs throughout the entire organization. It's an organization that has been designed with EX at its heart. And not all of it had to be created; it's organic to the founder's values and personality. However, the concepts of chaos, flexibility, and commitment have been implemented with intentionality, and that reflects design thinking through a concept we refer to as the *lens*.

Lenses are the different perspectives on an organization's EX that managers and leaders adopt and consider consciously. They allow leaders to view the EX from multiple points of view—to put on various hats and understand the beliefs and expectations of their employees through whatever frame is most helpful to the organization's success. The most effective leaders are those who can (and are willing to) go beyond their limited perspectives and see the EX with new eyes.

There are three lenses:

1. **Organizational Lens™.** Looking through this lens, the owner, executive, or manager sees the EX as it affects the organization: sales, market share, recruitment, partnerships, turnover, competition,

brand, personnel decisions, patient satisfaction, and more. When you view EX through the organizational lens, it's from the perspective of what is best for the organization, not necessarily the employees. Looking through this lens can help leaders temporarily set aside personal relationships and emotional issues related to employees to see what needs to be done to preserve the well-being of the organization. After all, while the organization doesn't exist without its employees, it works the other way around, too. It's tough to be employed by an organization that doesn't exist.

2. **Employee Lens™.** Looking through this lens, the leader sees the EX from the perspective of the employee. This is a way to get employees'-eye views of issues like compensation, engagement, culture, beliefs, and work-life balance. Using the employee lens, a manager might understand how employee beliefs led to a specific outcome in a way that wasn't possible had she looked at things only from her own perspective. Gazing through the employee lens provokes a manager to ask "How does this decision impact employees and their perceptions? How will *they* see it?"
3. **Leadership Lens™.** Looking through the lens of the leader means being able to look through the organizational and employee lenses at the same time, giving both views their appropriate consideration, while also paying attention to the leader's own viewpoint. This ability to look through multiple lenses is a skill found in elite leaders who are able to integrate three points of view: their own, the organization's, and employees'. Peering through the leader lens gives a broader, more complete range of insights needed to make decisions—but it doesn't tell them which decisions are best.

The lenses are tools for information gathering. They don't impart judgment, good or poor. These lenses are only as effective as the fairness, clarity, empathy, predictability, transparency, and accountability of the people doing the looking. They are powerful tools for intentionally designing, building, and shaping an organization and culture, but the outcome depends entirely on what you do with what you see.

Shifting between lenses, and asking questions through these lenses as guides, gives us a multiscopic, more complete perspective of expectations.

EGGHEAD ALERT!

The Mind-blinded Leader

Succeeding as leaders (or as members of society, in general) depends largely on our ability to see and interpret the perspectives and cues of those around us. Looking through different lenses—seeing ourselves in others' shoes—is referred to by psychologists as "Theory of Mind," as it is about forming theories or ideas of others' mental states or views.

Autism (from the Greek *autos*, which means "self") and Asperger's syndrome are developmental disorders characterized by significant difficulties in social interaction. In adults with autism or Asperger's, this ability to see through the lenses of others is severely impaired. This cognitive disorder is referred to as "mind-blindedness."[6]

Organizational Lens Questions
(from the Organization's Perspective)

1. Is this aspect of the EX consistent with the mission, culture, values, and direction of the organization or team?
2. Is it harmful or beneficial to our success as an organization or team and to our stakeholders, and if so, why?
3. How would changing this aspect of the EX impact engagement, beliefs, expectations, and relationships?
4. Would the benefits outweigh the potential detriments? Why or why not?

Employee Lens Questions
(from the Employee's Perspective)

1. How does this aspect of the EX align with my own expectations and beliefs as an employee of the company?
2. How does it impact trust and the perception that the organization or team keeps its promises?
3. Would changing this aspect of the EX be beneficial or detrimental to me personally and professionally? Why or why not?
4. Should I and other employees have a role or a voice in this? If not, why not? If yes, what should my/our role be?

Leadership Lens Questions
(Questions that Balance Multiple Perspectives)

1. How do organizational and employee views of the EX sync with the overall vision and mission of the organization or team?
2. What is most important right now to our success?
3. How can the needs of both the organization and the employees be served, and how do I as an individual leader within this organization personally view the intersection of these needs?
4. If all views cannot be aligned, how can we minimize negative consequences?

BECOMING MINDFUL AND DELIBERATE

Often, organizations develop inadvertently, pulled one way or the other by events, opportunities, crises, and happenstance. Without a clear vision and direction to guide that development, what comes out of that process is not culture but accident.

As we speak with employees across organizations and ask them "How would you describe the culture here?," one of the most common replies is "We don't really have a culture." This is interesting, because employees who don't think their organization has a culture are actually speaking volumes about the culture: It is a weak one where expectations are not aligned or intentionally created. It certainly wasn't created by intentional design.

Every organization has a culture. It's a by-product of people coming together to engage in collective activity. But where did that culture come from? Who created it? How did it evolve? When left to evolve and shape on its own, with no clear, intentional design, culture is created by employees, customers, suppliers, and even the public. The trouble is, that culture may be completely different from the culture that is most conducive to success.

Our goal, and the goal of this book, is to give you the tools and insights to make your EX—and the DNA or source code of your entire organization—intentional. This culture should be the result of high awareness of your employees' beliefs, expectations, and engagement and your own biases, views, and vision. Of course, that's a tall order. The intentional framework to make that happen is what we call the *Contract*.

Note the use of the capital "C" in "Contract." That's intentional, as it's the Contract that defines whether Expectation Alignment (EA) occurs or not. We'll get into this in more depth later, but for for now it's important to understand that every relationship has a Contract—or, sometimes, numerous Contracts.

CONTROL EXPECTATIONS BY UNDERSTANDING YOUR CONTRACT

Let's look back at the hapless Chicago Transit Authority, where outraged riders were hit with double charges and poor customer service. This fiasco was a clear case of misaligned expectations. But what expectations? Were these somehow outlined on a document signed by both parties before each rider boarded? No. But when riders hop on a bus, they expect to board, pay their fare, reach their destination, and get off the bus. No hassles (other than the smelly armpits of the person next to them); just transportation. Pretty simple. It's a sort of Contract between rider and the transportation authority. But in this case, the Contract between the CTA and its riders, as well as the one between the CTA and its employees, was violated.

The Contract is a concept, a mental construct that we use to understand and tweak the expectations at stake in any relationship, whether it's business or personal. Every relationship has a Contract. The Contract is the totality of explicit and implicit expectations that define the operating rules of the relationship, whether we are aware of them or not. Manager to subordinate, spouse to spouse, student to teacher, company to customer—every relationship comes with a Contract.

> The Contract is the totality of explicit and implicit expectations that define the operating rules of the relationship. Every relationship has a Contract.

The Contract is a perceived set of promises that establishes the terms of that relationship. Some Contracts are explicit, such as a written statement of work from a vendor or the Contract you sign when your daughter breaks her third mobile phone. Others aren't openly or clearly expressed or agreed on. These Contracts are implicit. But, whether implicit or explicit, every relationship carries a Contract.

Contracts exist at the organizational level, at the division or functional level, at the team level, and on a personal level. Like human beings, Contracts come in every shape and size, and they have multiple contributors and beneficiaries. The Contract is a container for an employee's many expectations about his or her workplace experience. It distills those expectations down into a few easily expressed, all-encompassing ideas.

For example:

Mary L.'s Contract with Her Employer

- I'll be paid what I believe I'm worth. My manager cares about me on a personal level and wants me to succeed and to develop my professional talents.
- The company will support me while I go for my graduate degree.
- The company will reward me for innovative ideas that help our customers.
- I will have a chance to advance to a management position within five years.
- I'll be able to dress as I please, so long as it's appropriate.
- This will always be a fun, informal place to work.
- The company will always behave responsibly toward the environment.
- We'll never downsize.

But management's Contract with Mary expresses those expectations in a very different way.

Management's Contract with Mary L.

"Provided that Mary continues to meet expectations for performance and conduct, we will pay her graduate school tuition, offer her incentives for good performance, offer a clear path to advancement, pay her at market value, and continue to reflect the values she cares about to the best of our ability."

Lots of qualifiers and room for misunderstanding in that sentence, aren't there? There should be. The Contract is where employee expectations meet the hard realities of running a complex organization and satisfying stakeholders. A nearly limitless variety of factors—some reasonable, some less so—impact the Contract, from the options package at a competitor company to marriages, births, and divorces. The Contract contains the promises that an organization can be reasonably expected to keep (e.g., no organization can be expected to promise that it will never downsize). On the other side, it implies that in order to get what they believe they deserve, employees must keep up their end of the bargain.

Around our offices, we've started to discuss the Contract when talking about what our employees expect from us and what we're expected to deliver. It's not uncommon to hear one of us say, "Was such-and-such part of our Contract with that person?" That's a useful check on our own actions, as well as a call to be ultra-aware of what we may have led our people to believe, intentionally or otherwise.

This double-check forces us to look through the leader lens. Sometimes it might be something as simple as listening attentively to a subordinate's ideas. It doesn't matter. If we've learned anything from our research for this book, it's that while there are reasonable and unreasonable expectations, there are no trivial ones.

While there are reasonable and unreasonable expectations, there are no trivial ones.

THE CONTRACT IS MUCH MORE THAN WORDS ON PAPER

Often, the Contract is both written (express or explicit) and unwritten (implicit), but the unwritten version is no less important than an agreement set down on paper. Think about the unwritten rules of baseball. There's a thick rulebook, but there's also a long list of things that players, coaches, and umpires know to be permissible. There's also another mental list of no-nos. Stealing the other team's base-running signs or signals is frowned on but accepted. Heaving a fastball at a batter who admires a home run for too long? That's okay . . . until you throw at his head.

There's an unspoken agreement based on mutual trust that neither side will take things to excess, and it changes based on game circumstances and the players involved. Break an explicit rule and you get penalized or thrown out of the game. Break some of the implied rules, and you won't get ejected, but you're not likely to have a long career.

The Contract hinges on four questions that all organizational leaders—executives, managers, church leaders, head coaches, hospital administrators, and college deans—must ask:

1. Are we creating clear, reasonable, aligned expectations for our people that contribute to our mutual well-being?
2. How are our employees translating our expectations into individual, personal beliefs and promises?
3. Which employee expectations are reasonable and realistic and which are not?
4. Are our choices, words, and actions fulfilling or violating employee expectations?

Every relationship, from a company to a marriage or a parent and child, forms around a core of explicit and implied expectations. The health of the relationship depends in great part on whether the expectations are legitimate and realistic and whether the parties live up to what's expected and earn trust. That's why clarity is critical. In the Contract, both parties have to be clear about what they're agreeing to and what is simply off the table.

By the way, our mention of marriages and parenting is no accident. The Contract may center on organizations, such as for-profit corporations, healthcare organizations, universities, business teams, and nonprofits, but the interplay between expectations and trust applies everywhere, from families to sports teams to churches to the military. Where there are people, there are Contracts.

WHY IS THE CONTRACT LIKE AN ICEBERG?

This question sounds like one from the Riddler, from the 1960s *Batman* TV series, doesn't it? "Riddle me this, Caped Crusader! Why is a contract like an iceberg?" If you're not familiar with that television classic starring Adam West, stop what you're doing and find it on YouTube. Seriously. We'll wait.

Pop culture references aside, Contracts are essential to a civilized society. Practically every aspect of daily life, from the house you live in and the car you drive to the cable television you watch at the end of a long day, brings with it a Contract that guarantees or incentivizes a certain behavior. You sign Contracts promising to make payments on a mortgage or auto loan, pay your cable or Hulu bill, drive your motor vehicles lawfully, and vote only once in any election, among many others. So it makes sense that contract law makes up the majority of the first-year curriculum at most law schools.

As a first-year law student learns, a Contract has three basic parts:

1. The *offer*, in which one party agrees to do something in return for the other party agreeing to do something else.
2. *Acceptance*, in which the other party indicates they agree to what is being offered and the terms under which it's being offered.
3. The *consideration*, which refers to something of legal value (whether larger or small) given up or exchanged that makes the agreement something more than a mere promise. You might think of consideration as the reason you are entering into the contract. "I give you money, and you give me ESPN on channel 142."

When these basic elements exist, you have a Contract that is enforceable, rather than an arrangement that is more akin to your shallow promise to pay for lunch the next time around.

A promise that is enforceable is powerful. Because of the power of Contracts we all spend a great deal of time and money drafting, revising, making, and fighting about them. Whenever there is a dispute, the question is whether there was a meeting of the minds: "What was agreed on?" The answer to that question is simple, right? Just look at the written Contract. Okay, not so fast . . .

Offer and acceptance represent alignment: "What have we agreed on?" But Contracts quickly become more complex than mutual agreement. The written, or express (explicit), aspect of a Contract, for all its dense legal folderol, is the easy part. It clearly and precisely defines the parties, terms, prohibitions, time frames, and other essentials of any agreement between parties, and spells out who's giving what to whom. At their core, Contracts are about aligning and managing expectations.

Nearly all disputes that occur in connection with a Contract arise due to one of three causes:

1. Expectations were not clearly established or understood from the beginning.
2. Expectations were not met.
3. Expectations were not properly aligned and managed.

The problem is that not every expectation makes its way into the written Contract. The implied part of any Contract is what carries the weight of the subconscious, unspoken expectations that each party brings to the relationship. These implied Contracts are the type your grandfather meant when he talked about doing business based on a handshake back in the day—nothing formal, other than a mutual belief that each party would act with the best interest of both sides at heart. With an implied Contract, there exists a tacit understanding—an awareness that's understood or implied without being stated—among all parties about the terms of the Contract and what is expected of everyone. Trust is everything. Without it, there's no deal.

So a Contract really is like an iceberg: You might see the written, express part bobbing above the water, but the larger part—the *implied* part—is submerged. The implied component is the most important section of any Contract, and that's where things can go sideways. This is where Expectation Alignment Dysfunction runs rampant.

In law, you do your best to draft a Contract that covers all contingencies, but for all practical purposes, that's impossible. At the end of the day, the Contract isn't the one you put on paper; it's the Contract that people *think* they agreed to. Everybody might be happy on the day they sign, but two years later their expectations and view of the Contract's fairness can change completely. That's what keeps attorneys in business.

Take, for example, the case of a retail store's relationship with a customer. The customer insists that the store didn't deliver her product within the agreed upon time frame, and that it's not the quality that she had anticipated. Basically, it won't meet her needs. As the store looks at the written Contract, it realizes they goofed. Sure enough, it was a day late. But it shouldn't have been a big deal, the delivery people reason—the customer postponed delivery several times.

That said, the customer is clearly wrong about the product quality. She got exactly what she ordered. If she wanted the better product, she should have gone with the next model up. At least, that's what the delivery people think.

The customer phones the firm, and really lays into them. She tells the firm they are wrong, citing the conversation she had with the salesperson where she clearly outlined her needs. The delivery people, along with the salesperson, pull out the signed contract. While the salesperson remembers the conversation and the customer explaining her needs, the contract in front of them clearly tells them they delivered the correct item.

But the customer doesn't see it that way. She is fixated on the late delivery and the fact that she trusted the salesperson to understand and resolve her product needs.

So, who is right? The truth is, it doesn't matter—at least to the relationship.

Similarly, when we step into the world of employer-employee relationships, we forge Contracts that are even more complex than a retail agreement or those used on Wall Street. The implicit, unstated components of these contracts are enormous in size and scope and as potentially dangerous as that icebeg was to the *Titanic*.

Consider this: How important are our working lives to our hopes, dreams, and identities? For many of us, our working life is one of our greatest expressions of our creativity, purpose, and aspirations for the future. After all, we spend most of our waking hours at work. Because of this, our relationships at work, whether with our boss, employees, peers, customers, or others, have tremendous impact on our health and well-being.

Each of these relationships comes with its own Contract, and most of the terms of those Contracts are implicit, not spelled out. That means those implied Contracts—and the relationships they depend on—are both more ephemeral and more perilous than anything printed up by a bank or enforced by a court. That's why it's so important to understand what's beneath the surface. It's where the three lenses come into play. Only when you look at a relationship from the perspectives of everyone involved can you manage it to its fullest expression.

THE EXPECTATION TRIANGLE

Another reality about expectations and Contracts is that they are never static. The Contract is always being created, reinforced, or violated. Every action leaders take, no matter how innocuous, has one of these three effects on the Contract—sometimes with just one employee, sometimes with all of them.

Let's go back to the big $70,000 pay announcement from Gravity Payments. If the CEO told a small circle of employees about his plan before the announcement, his message reinforced their expectation that he would follow through. For most of the others, he created a brand-new expectation. And for the few who felt betrayed that less senior employees would earn the same salaries as they did, Price's action actually violated their Contract (and Gravity is currently dealing with the fallout of this perceived violation).

Within each Contract are layers and layers of subtleties that demand a great deal of attention and mindfulness. What reinforces one employee's Contract might breach another's. It depends on the circumstances. That's why it's so crucial for leaders to be aware of employee expectations, reasonable or not. Being oblivious to them, especially when an organization is experiencing radical changes, is like ignoring a ticking bomb in your midst. If you're up to speed on what people expect, you might not be able to keep a resentment bomb from going off, but you can contain the damage.

THREE CONTRACTS IN ONE

Contracts are inherently problematic and incomplete. So why do we offer them as tools to help foster EA? We aren't talking about using typed documents. We are suggesting that you use Contracts as devices for establishing, understanding, managing, and aligning employee expectations.

As we explained, every relationship is based on a Contract, but there's more to it. Every Contract is actually made up of three subcontracts, which we'll cover in greater depth in subsequent chapters. The three subcontracts are:

1. **Brand Contract.** The Brand Contract is how we are viewed publicly or are seen by others. It consists of the promises that our brand identity—what we profess to be and what we stand for as an organization or team—makes to the people who are exposed to it.
2. **Transactional Contract.** The Transactional Contract is the mutually accepted, reciprocal, and explicit agreement between two or more entities that defines the basic operating terms of the relationship.
3. **Psychological Contract.** The Psychological Contract is the unwritten, implicit set of expectations and obligations that define the terms of exchange in a relationship.

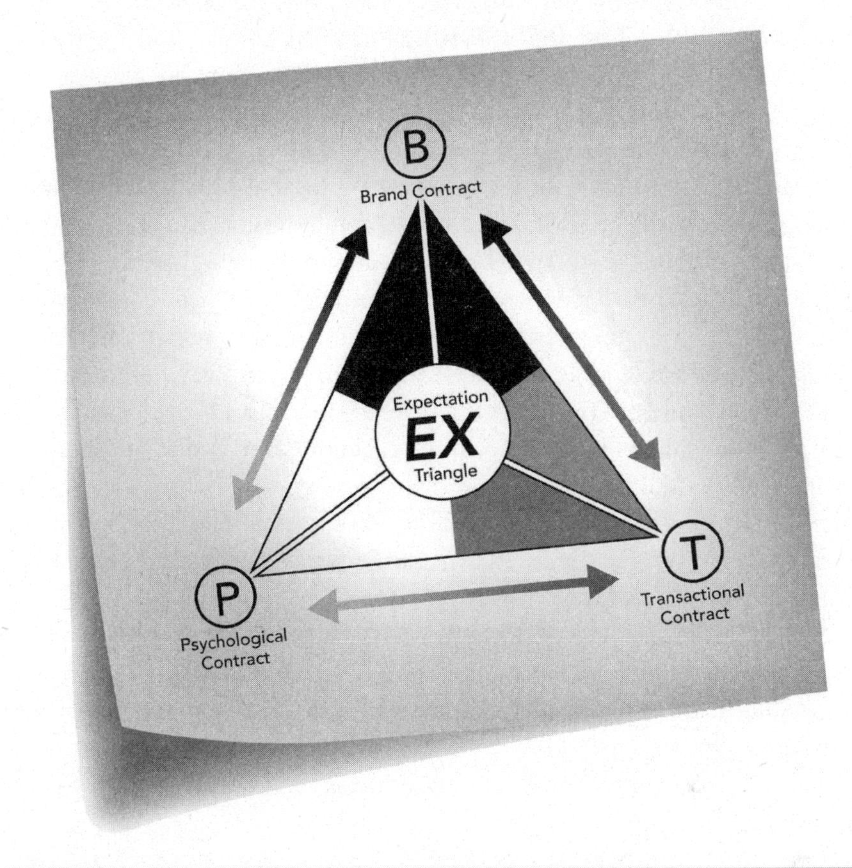

FIGURE 4.1 The Contract Expectation Triangle

We threw these brief definitions out there as a teaser for something critical we found in our research; there are actually three Contracts inherent in your EX (and, in fact, in every relationship). The quality of every relationship is dependent upon whether expectations set by these three contracts align (Figure 4.1). Ultimately, these three contracts—the Brand Contract, the Transactional Contract, and the Psychological Contract—determine the quality of the Employee Experience.

So, if you'd like to gain a better understanding of how to attract talent, retain top performers, and drive business results, join us on our journey through the land of the three Contracts.

CHAPTER 4. AN INTENTIONAL FRAMEWORK: THE CHAPTER EXPERIENCE

- Each stakeholder in the organization is a custodian of a different part of the EX.
- Design thinking is the underlying developmental philosophy behind EA. It starts with the goal of creating a solution, not fixing a problem, and keeps people—in this case, employees—at the center of everything.
- Lenses are the three perspectives through which you should view your EX. The organizational lens looks at the EX based on what's right for the whole. The employee lens looks at the EX based on the beliefs and expectations of the employee. The leader lens looks at both simultaneously while also taking into account the leader's individual perspective.
- The Contract represents the collective expectations of a relationship—a set of explicit and implicit expectations that define the operating rules of that relationship.
- Every relationship has a Contract, whether we are aware of it or not.
- The Contract is like an iceberg: Although you see the obvious written agreement, there's a lot more below the surface that's unspoken but just as important.
- Contracts are never static. They are always in the process of being reinforced, violated, or changed.
- There are three kinds of subcontracts that make up the overall Contract: Brand, Transactional, and Psychological.

Three Contracts

CHAPTER 5

The Brand Contract

I alone cannot change the world, but I can cast a stone across the waters to create many ripples.

—Mother Teresa

On October 27, 2015, $2.2 billion outdoor recreation specialty retailer REI sent a letter to its 5.5 million co-op members: It would be closing its stores on Black Friday, the biggest shopping day of the year. More than that, the company would give all of its 12,000 employees a paid holiday so they could get outside and enjoy nature, something at the heart of the REI message. Later, as the November 27 national "shop 'til you drop" fiesta grew closer, the company released a national television commercial about the shutdown featuring the Twitter hashtag #OptOutside and launched a website, www.optoutside.rei.com, where users could find trail suggestions and other outdoor recreation ideas.

It was a major doubling down on brand identity and promise . . . and a big risk. Did it pay off? By all accounts, the answer is a resounding "You bet your hiking boots!" Apart from garnering REI enormous press coverage, the Black Friday closure boosted the company's online sales on November 27 by 26 percent.[1] Over 1,408,000 people joined the campaign on the company's social media channels.

But more important, REI branded itself as the instigator of a movement and an ongoing conversation about consumerism and recreation. The decision was a full-throated shout of authenticity backing up the co-op's stated values—bold and trust-building support of REI's Contract with its customers and employees. Everything began, as it should have, with the employees.

In the eyes of the public, REI went overnight from a much-loved outfitter to one of the rare companies where values and purpose are as important as, if not more important than, short-term profit. It became one of the good guys, real and trustworthy. For years, REI branding and culture had stated "This is who we are. This is what we stand for." With #OptOutside, REI walked that talk. It fulfilled its Brand Contract.

WHAT IS THE BRAND CONTRACT?

We begin our look at the three subcontracts that make up the heart of what we defined as the Contract with the Brand Contract. It's the first one your employees come into contact with. How is that possible? Well, think about what the Brand Contract is:

> **Your Brand Contract is all the implied promises that your brand makes to the people who are exposed to it.**

The world operates in an economy where brand is everything. Organizations are always trying to build, enhance, and defend their brands, and they'll all tell you that the brand represents a set of promises made to the consumer. Apple's brand promises peerless product design. Tesla's brand promises to reinvent the car and the car-buying experience. Home Depot promises that you'll find everything you need under one roof and the expertise to get the job done. But when we began this decades-long love affair with the brand, we forgot that the brand's promise affects employees, too.

Your Brand Contract consists of everything that your culture, marketing, reputation, media coverage, and the behavior of your people do to create expectations. It's your public face—the way the world sees your organization. What makes this Contract tricky to manage is that it can (and will) affect employee expectations before employees even *become* employees.

One of the most critical pieces to understand about the Brand Contract is that it plays a significant role in a potential new hire's desire to join your organization (or your team). And this is where perks play an important role.

Potential recruits may be enticed by the onsite gym, snack bar, high pay, and your cafeteria, or by the reputation your company has in the community. Is that a bad thing? Certainly not. In fact, perks, benefits, and reputation are essential in remaining competitive in the recruiting market.

Then there's the customer. If your customer is the young, hip crowd, your brand should reflect a tone that attracts that kind of employee. Perks are one of the many pieces that go into creating that atmosphere. While Nerf gun wars and guitar-playing hippies in cubicles may be exactly what a tech company desires, a medical or law office may look more to perks like opportunities to attend conferences or professional lunches. Your Brand Contract, whether it be a Contract with the entire organization or within your own team, should be in line with the customers you are serving, the people you want to attract, and the type of service or product you hope to deliver.

Your brand may bring people aboard, but it doesn't mean they will engage, and will likely not keep them from jumping ship if something more appealing comes along. Understand, however, that the brand your organization puts forward—whether positive or negative—often determines whether people will want to be a part of that relationship.

How's that again? We'll explain. Say Olivia responds to your online posting for an open position. Before she even comes in for the interview, she's already Googled your company, read your company's online reviews, talked to her neighbor, and gone to your website. She likes the idea of working for a firm that values expertise and professionalism, and is impressed by what she sees when she looks into your company. She's already formed an impression of who you are, how you operate, and what you value, so she already has expectations for her Employee Experience (EX), should she get the job. Making the situation even more slippery is that she *might not even realize* that she has formed these expectations. But *you* should. It's the leader's role to account for the *a priori* effect that the brand can have on potential hires so they can:

1. Understand the employer brand as it is perceived both outside and inside the organization.
2. Adjust the message the organization is sending out through its brand and communications to avoid creating unrealistic expectations.
3. Account for this "priming" in the recruitment process and counter any problematic expectations new hires might develop.

> Your Brand Contract consists of everything that your culture, marketing, reputation, media coverage, and the behavior of your people do to create expectations. It's your public face—the way the world sees you.

UNANTICIPATED CONSEQUENCES

What makes the Brand Contract as perilous as it is loaded with potential is how little organizational leaders know about it. For one thing, its influence doesn't stop when someone is hired. An organization's brand continues to be a force in its internal culture, and that brand continues to exert influence on each person's perception of what to expect from the future. So it's not enough to be aware of how your messaging and online presence are impacting your recruiting pool; you must keep tabs on how media coverage and the internal ebb and flow of politics and relationships affect current personnel.

Reflect back on Amazon. The company never promised a heartwarming experience. But it did promise to add heft to the professional experience section of your résumé and put an above-average wage in your pocket. Wrong or right, it stayed true to its promise, even amid a barrage of negative media.

Under most circumstances, when the Contract is agreed to by both parties, the terms are set, and renegotiating them means that the existing Contract must be torn up and a new one worked out in its place. But the Brand Contract is subject to constant renegotiation (this generally doesn't involve an explicit agreement) based on ongoing experiences, making it unlike any other type of Contract. The Brand Contract has to adapt because it's based on how the organization evolves in real time.

For example, when a company launches, it might be fast-acting and financially independent, so part of its Brand Contract is that it's an agile, free-thinking rebel. Once it grows and files an IPO, it's subject to the laws and scrutiny that affect public corporations, so it can't be as free and easy. It must become more conservative and safeguard information more carefully. As it adapts, so does its Brand Contract with employees. As long as employees understand why that evolution is taking place, there probably will be few objections.

Another point of interest is that the Brand Contract is subject to influences that are completely out of your control: Twitter, articles in *BusinessWeek* and *Fast Company*, conversations at professional conferences or in the local Starbucks, even your brother-in-law's loudmouth opinion. Your brand is subject to so many outside factors that the forces you *can* control become all the more important. You may not be able to control what people say or write about your organization, but you can influence it by being transparent and consistent about your values, mission, and behavior—by making sure that your public face syncs up with your private actions.

When Olivia is hired, she is handed an employment Contract (this is the Transactional Contract, which we'll cover later on) that sets down in detail what she can expect from her job. However, as her employment continues, her expectations and EX gradually hinge less on the details of the written Contract, and more and more on perceptions: how the company is changing, what people are saying, and so on.

Olivia's Brand Contract began with perceptions carried by the news, industry gossip, social media, and so on, creating a sort of "imaginary" organization that Olivia thinks she would love to work for. Then she's hired and, over time, facts replace perceptions as she discovers what the organization is really like. We see the same thing on dating websites like Match.com. A photo, description, and a few emails might create an idealized version of a person based on excited expectations. Then you go on a date and—for better or worse—idealism and fantasy becomes reality.

Whether reality supports or contradicts the expectations created by the Brand Contract has a lot to do with what the employee's experience will be like. It's easy to see how a public brand that's severely at odds with the reality of working for an organization might lead to serious disillusionment and disengagement.

THE EMPLOYEE VALUE PROPOSITION

In August 2015, much of the world was tense, due to stock market chaos and the international financial situation. Starbucks chairman and CEO Howard Schultz, in what some called inspired leadership and others called a bizarre move, issued a memo to the chain's 190,000 "partners" (Starbuck-speak for "employees"). In it, Schultz asked partners to be "very sensitive" to what customers might be feeling. The memo states:

> Our company has weathered many different types of storms. But our brand has never been stronger or more relevant. Our pipeline of new products and breakthrough innovation has never been more robust. And our long term commitment to delivering an elevated partner experience is unwavering. I can assure you

that we will continue to lead and manage the company through the lens of humanity, doing everything we possibly can to continue to make your families proud of our company and all we stand for. You have my word on this.[2]

Notice the intentional, careful wording as the firm's chief barista reiterates the brand: strong, relevant, new products, innovation, robust, long-term commitment, elevated partner experience, unwavering, lead, manage, lens of humanity, families, proud, we stand for, my word. These words were likely not chosen lightly, as they highlight the company's brand and value proposition.

Every organization has a customer value proposition. Schultz identifies a piece of it later in the memo by describing a "unique in-store experience" and "highly relevant coffee and tea innovation and differentiatied customer-facing digital technologies." Organizations make brand promises to their customer base—the highest standard of cancer care, 98 percent job placement after graduation, the longest-lasting minty flavor, the juiciest burger, and so on. Consumers make their purchases based on how well the value proposition aligns with their interests and expectations. When Expectation Alignment (EA) occurs (what I want and expect as a consumer aligns with what you propose you will provide), you get an expanding customer base and repeat business.

Since your brand impacts your employees as well, there is also an Employee Value Proposition (EVP). Just as the customer has expectations around a firm's brand, so does an employee. While the Customer Value Proposition defines the value of a firm's products or services to the consumer, the Employee Value Proposition (a subset of your Brand Contract) is the value—tangible, intangible, and reputational—that an employee receives from an organization in exchange for his or her work.

When we work with organizations around their employee engagement initiatives, we often conduct what we refer to as "engagement summits." During these summits, we review the results of the company's employee engagement surveys, discuss recommendations for improvement, and develop action plans. One of the key components of these summits is to discuss the organization's EVP.

We start by asking leaders "Why would someone choose to work for you?" All but the most in-touch organizations come back with reponses like "We pay above market," "We were just voted an employer of choice," "We have a recognizable name," or simply "Because we have a lot of open positions." Others simply look at each other, laugh uncomfortably, and say "We have no idea." Regardless, few are able to look through the employee lens to describe their EVP in any level of detail. Those who can articulate their EVP find they are able to take advantage of their Brand Contract in both recruiting and retention.

We worked with two restaurant companies, one a 400-location fast food chain and the other a 150-location upscale chain. The fast food employees, as we learned through surveys and focus groups, found the greatest value in flexible schedules (which allowed them to meet family, school, and social obligations), the ability to associate with friends while on the job, and getting 50 percent off of one-per-week lunches (a perk that cost about 78 cents per week per employee). The upscale restaurant workers, in contrast, were engaged by completely different factors: opportunities for growth, development, and advancement; the trust of their managers; community support; and satisfied customers.

The leaders at the fast food chain, understanding their EVP, also understood that most of their workers were young and mobile-device savvy. In order to facilitate scheduling (one of the key drivers of their value proposition), they went to an app-based scheduling system their employees could access from home. They implemented a recruiting referral program that paid employees $100 per referral hired and had networks of friends and family working together in the same locations. They expanded their discounted food program to include one meal per four-hour shift. Employee engagement and retention increased significantly.

The upscale food chain also looked at its EVP and discovered that the value proposition varied across job descriptions. For example, we discovered that a large percentage of the chain's servers (who made up a significant portion of the population) fit into one of two categories: students and single parents. For them, flexible schedules with sufficient working hours to pay the bills was extremely important. The restaurants accommodated. Restaurant managers and assistant managers, however, valued the opportunity for career development, training, and advancement. The organization put in place a comprehensive leadership training program that addressed these expectations—a great example of seeing things through the leader lens.

Understanding your EVP helps you answer the following two-part questions:

1. What is our organization's brand?
   So, what are the outcomes of having that brand?
2. Why would someone choose to *join* this organization (what is the value we propose to future employees)?
   So, what would it take to attract that person?
3. Why would an employee choose to *stay* at this organization?
   So, what would it take to keep that person?
4. Do we have Expectation Gaps or Expectation Alignment in our Brand Contract?
   So, what would it take to close any gaps?

Back to Starbucks. In his memo, Schultz also states the chain is "making a profound social impact in the communities we serve." The memo goes on to say:

> The experience we deliver in our stores, the strength and equity of our brand, and the primary reason for our current and future success is because of all of YOU. I believe in you and have never been prouder to be your partner.

For those whose values and expectations align with this brand, they are likely to find Starbucks the perfect environment, whether they're digging the java or just buzzed about their jobs.

> The Employee Value Proposition is the value an employee receives from an organization in exchange for the employee's work.

WHAT DEFINES THE BRAND CONTRACT

The Brand Contract is your organizational weather. It rains or shines on your customers and their needs, as well as on your EVP. It doesn't determine everything that happens from day to day, but it does set the underlying conditions and prepares the ground. In a way, the Brand Contract decides what you *can't* do as much as what you can. For instance, let's say that for the first five years of your tech company's existence, you have cultivated a brand that's painted you as a bold, creative, rule-breaking innovator. Creative geniuses flock to your door. But that's not working; you're losing money, and the future is in doubt.

You try to make a radical shift and adopt a more conservative, fiscally prudent, slow-growth business model. But you can't, at least not with the people you have. Your Brand Contract has attracted recruits who fit your wild-and-crazy identity and encourages them to throw caution to the wind after being hired. Your team values that type of free-spirit environment. But you can't keep going down this path. Wacky, off-the-wall ideas are great, but you're having a tough time getting any of these ideas to market.

You don't have any conservative financial minds or operations strategists on board. So, you just go on a hiring binge, right? Not so fast. Remember your EVP? Remember why this group of rebels joined your organization in the first place? Following after the Brand Contract is a *brand wake*, a time lag that, like the wake from a passing ship, continues to influence beliefs and expectations, even after you've turned your organization in a new direction. So you might post job listings and get the word out that your company is now a cautious, customer-focused operation. (You've changed your EVP.) But as far as everyone knows, including your employees, you're still the same wild child that gave out a monthly Best Tattoo award. No matter how fast you turn the ship, that wake is still influencing your value proposition, how people see your company, who applies for open positions, and whether your current employees feel comfortable staying or not.

Your EVP and the length of time your organization has been traveling in that direction determine how strong and long your brand wake is. Beliefs change slowly. But your EVP is only one of the forces that defines your Brand Contract. Others might include:

- **Reputation.** What do the news media, your peers, your neighbor, and the person on the street say about your organization?
- **Organizational communication.** Every bit of content you put out, from your website to your press releases to your employee handbook, shapes beliefs and expectations.
- **Values.** Is there a set of publicly proclaimed values that guide how your organization is run? What are they, and do you follow them consistently or only when it's convenient?
- **Leadership personas.** The CEO, senior executives, and other managers are the face of the organization in the media and at professional

events. How do they conduct themselves publicly? What message do they send with their words, appearance, behavior, and body language? This applies at the team or department level as well. What reputation does your team have? What reputation do you have as a manager?

- **Culture.** What does working in your organization feel like? That's culture in a nutshell. The nature of your culture (fun, intense, rebellious, high-tech, high performing), whether it feels intentional or accidental, and how well it serves its main goal—helping your employees engage fully and perform at their best—has a lot to do with your Brand Contract.
- **Authenticity.** Does what the organization says and does feel forced and artificial, or like the work of real people?
- **Openness.** Do you respond to customers on social media, encourage candid feedback from employees, and deal in truth, not spin?
- **Customers.** Who receives your services or buys your products? Changing from a private school known for STEM education to a charter school aimed at fine arts dramatically changes your customer base. Is this what you want?

We know that's an impossibly long list of factors to track and manage, but don't panic. The organizations that have been the most successful at building a solid Brand Contract—one that reinforces the beliefs and expectations they want—have done it by focusing on being authentic, driven by deep values, open and honest with their people, and consistent in what they do and say to everyone. In other words, they've been good human beings first, good leaders second.

Which brings up an important point. It's not just the organization that has a brand. Each individual manager location, and even departments and functions have their own brands, which may or may not line up with the organization's brand.

It's quite possible that your organization has a stellar brand and has honored that Contract to the letter. Yet your best employee in the customer care department sees her boss toss the organization's Brand Contract aside. "Great company," she thinks, "but this guy's a real jerk." Although we won't spend much time on this fact, it's important to understand a manager's individual role in brand creation and protection. Just be warned: In a situation like this, your number-one customer care team member will probably go elsewhere.

WHAT THE BRAND CONTRACT DOES

For more than 30 years, Patagonia, a Ventura, California–based outdoor clothing company, has built its brand as much on environmental responsibility as on quality products and service. In 2011, the company startled the world and shook the apparel industry by running an ad campaign that encouraged its customers not to buy its clothing and to recycle their old Patagonia items to reduce their overall environmental footprint. Crazy? Maybe, but leading with their corporate values paid off for the progressive, family-oriented, privately held Patagonia. In 2012, the year after it began its "cause marketing" campaign, sales jumped by nearly a third, to $543 million.[3]

Patagonia has led with its heart and environmental commitment ever since founder Yvon Chouinard launched the company in 1973. The company engages in practices that might make other clothing companies go pale.

The company pioneered onsite day care for its employees. It has made its supply chain public by using an online map to show every farm, textile mill, and factory it uses in sourcing its materials and manufacturing its products. It's one of the founding organizations behind the One Percent for the Planet initiative, in which participating companies donate 1 percent of their total sales to environmental causes. It offers its people "environmental internships" that allow them two months of leave with full pay and benefits to work at an environmental nonprofit of their choice. And famously, its coastal headquarters often shuts down on days when the Ventura surf is inviting.

As you might expect, this unbelievably employee-friendly, values-first culture breeds not only ferocious employee loyalty and microscopic turnover but a Brand Contract whose values align perfectly with the company's EVP. That's what happens when you honor expectations.

When you violate the Brand Contract, though, employees conclude that the organization's promises are little more than window dressing designed to attract customers. It's a few short steps from there to being perceived as hypocritical, and hypocrisy does not earn loyalty. In short:

Honoring the Brand Contract = Commitment

Violating the Brand Contract = Disloyalty

A MECHANISM FOR EXPECTATION ALIGNMENT

Take a look through the employee lens. Think about how regularly and radically circumstances can change in any organization and how severely some changes can affect what employees perceive as the promises made to them.

A nonprofit might lose a major donor and have to cut its budget. A hospital might be subject to a massive class action lawsuit. A university could face budget problems and be forced to let some nontenured faculty go. Or a new supervisor could simply come into a department, dislike the fast-and-loose way things have been done, and institute a system designed to restore order at the expense of fun. Change can have a thousand faces, and most of them are disruptive, even if they are positive.

Even positive changes can disturb expectations in negative ways. At Gravity Payments, Wal-Mart, and other companies, employees have quit after across-the-board raises were announced.[4] Why? These employees didn't like the idea that less senior people were receiving raises they didn't deserve. Change is hard under the best of circumstances, and even beneficial changes in an organization can make employees feel that the rules are being ignored or the ground is shifting under their feet.

Through all this, the Brand Contract can serve as the anchor for employee expectations and keep EA relatively high. Sure, we said earlier that the Brand Contract is subject to change, but in circumstances only. The Brand Contract must have three anchors:

1. The values that have personal meaning to those in leadership roles—integrity, helping the less fortunate, wellness, or whatever those values might be.
2. The sense of mission behind the organization—what you're trying to accomplish in the world.
3. Authentically caring about people, starting with your employees.

As long as these three pieces of the Brand Contract are explicit and don't change, the rest of the organization can grow quickly, shift direction, or go into survival mode, and most employees will feel like they still have some solid ground to rest their feet on. They will still believe that the organization and its leaders are meeting (or planning to meet) their expectations.

Take cloud computing firm Salesforce. A new employee at Salesforce may find himself working at a public park, rather than in the office, on his first day at work. That's because one of the firm's stated goals is "giving back." It's part of the Salesforce brand. During the orientation period for each new hire, he or she will provide a certain amount of volunteer service, including picking out produce for a local food bank, working at a school or shelter, or rebuilding wildlife habitat. And these opportunities for service continue throughout an employee's tenure at the company.

Salesforce takes a "1–1–1" approach to philanthropy and volunteerism. It gives 1 percent of its products, 1 percent of its equity, and 1 percent of employees' time to local nonprofits.[5] Ebony Frelix, who has headed up the firm's philanthropy and employee engagement efforts, claims, "It's part of our corporate DNA. It's why employees choose Salesforce, because we have that volunteer component."[6]

A day out of the office isn't a perk. It's a reflection of the organization's values. It's written into the Brand Contract. While the manner in which Salesforce exemplifies these values may change, and the way the company does business may change, it has built volunteerism and giving back into its EVP. They're values, and they represent a commitment to employees: *No matter what else changes, these values will remain the same.*

A well-managed Brand Contract maximizes Expectation Alignment by keeping the underlying fabric of the organization consistent while circumstances change.

HOW THE BRAND CONTRACT AFFECTS EX

We're not suggesting that organizational leaders and employees join hands and sing hymns. We are suggesting that leaders respect their people enough to level with them, trust them to handle challenging circumstances, and have a good explanation why if the firm can't keep a promise. "Walking the walk" should be considered the minimum requirement for a solid Brand Contract. But how do you know if your Brand Contract is solid? With the Brand Contract influenced by so many outside forces, can you keep your finger on its pulse and hope to feel anything like an accurate heartbeat?

Yes, but indirectly. You assess the health of your Brand Contract by putting on the leader lens, assessing EA, and looking at these indicators of your overall EX:

- **Investment in culture.** At its heart, a strong Brand Contract makes employees feel they are being rewarded for having the wisdom to place their trust in you. They feel safe. (That's why broken Contracts can become so toxic; they are a betrayal.) If your Brand Contract is sound, you will find that employees invest in your culture: participating in events, leading committees, and getting involved.
- **Defense of the organization.** It's easy to write something positive about any organization. What's more revealing is when a current employee—or a past one—comes to its defense on social media or on a review service like Yelp or Glassdoor. When you see this happening, your brand is evoking real loyalty.
- **Challenging the status quo.** We're not encouraging you to let employees defy directives. But in an environment where they feel safe and respected, employees should feel that they can challenge conventional thinking, ask their superiors tough questions, and expect substantive answers. If that's happening, smile.
- **Risk taking.** The same qualities—safety and respect—come into play in regard to risk taking. Strong, consistent culture and care for employees gives them the freedom to test boundaries and innovate without fear.

Note that these have nothing to do with perks or compensation. No company ever won hearts and minds with raises or pinball machines. The currency being traded is trust, communication, authenticity, and mutual respect—a Brand Contract that welcomes high expectations and meets them. Your employees become the rising tide that lifts all boats.

The phrase "this changes everything" is overused, but it's appropriate here. The power of the Brand Contract inverts the dynamic between employers and the employed. Traditionally, employers have demanded absolute loyalty from their employees without being expected to reciprocate. The EX was what the employer said it was.

No more. In the Age of the Employee, employers who want loyalty have to earn it by being worthy of trust and backing up their stated values with action.

Now, here's the catch. Contracts work both ways. If your employees aren't living up to their end of the Brand Contract, exemplifying your Brand in what they do, they might not belong in your organization or on your team.

A CANARY IN YOUR COAL MINE

Let's say you're not taking your cues from the Salesforces of the world. You're letting your Brand Contract mutate and change accidentally without thought for how this affects your EX. It's surprisingly easy for the Brand Contract to become an afterthought. It's so fluid, changeable, and subtle that it can't be worth all the attention and time it takes to manage it, right?

Wrong. It's the foundation of every other Contract you have with your people. It determines the value you propose to your team. So monitoring the health of your Brand Contract is crucial. It's like the canary in your organization's coal mine: If you see your Brand Contract starting to gasp for air, you can be sure that expectations are slipping out of alignment, the EX is suffering, and your Transactional and Psychological Contracts are hurting as well.

When your culture, values, or behavior start to differ from what your brand has promised employees in the past, you have a problem. Watch for these warning signs:

- **Degradation of your "recruiting brand."** Strong, clear brand and culture make recruitment more productive by making it easier to attract people who are well suited to your organization. When attracting them stops being easy, you may have a disconnect between brand promise and brand reality. You might start seeing messages like some of our favorites (courtesy of our Prospective Team Member Surveys) from applicants:
  - "The application process was a mess. The woman at the staffing agency told me your recruiting was disorganized, but I think she understated how crazy it would be."
  - "I was disappointed by [name]'s professionalism in the interview process. He told me twice that he would get back to me, then had his secretary send me a rejection notice after four weeks. I've had bad dates give me more considerate rejections. If this is the way you work with your clients, I was lucky not to be hired."

- "I would like to withdraw my application. After seeing the stunts your company just pulled in the media, I have no desire to be a part of that."
- "Your customer service manager told me I probably wouldn't get the job, then proceeded to try and recruit me for his own multi-level healthcare marketing scheme. Not only would I not work for your firm, I will go out of my way to tell people not to do business with your credit union."
- "Which company is this again?"

You don't need to see such ugly messages to have a broken recruitment brand. If you are seeing a slowdown in the number of applicants for open positions, if people are accepting jobs and then backing out before starting work, if your quality of new hires seems lower, or if your level of "fit" seems to be declining, you may have a damaged Brand Contract that's promising one thing but delivering another.

- **Reduced engagement.** Every organization should be conducting engagement surveys of its people, both formally and informally. If you do, and you see marked negative changes in engagement indicators from one survey to the next, and the next, that's a red flag that you may have issues with your Brand Contract. True, it can also be a harbinger of other problems, but lower engagement scores should get you looking critically at what your brand is saying to employees.

  Through our employee engagement surveys, we ask employees to rate the statement: "I would recommend this company to others as a great place to work." We find that for every six promoters (those responding "strongly agree" or "agree"), there is an average of one detractor (those responding with a "strongly disagree")—a 6:1 ratio.

  Research in the Customer Experience (CX) world parallels what we find in the EX world: Both promoters and detractors spread the word. This means that, on average, for every six ambassadors you have employed in your company, there is one employee doing what he or she can to tear your brand apart.

- **Increased focus on pay, benefits, and perks.** It's been proven time and again: When employees feel part of a larger purpose and that their employer shares their values, they care less about compensation, perks, and other "hygiene factors" (if you're unfamiliar with this term, be patient—we'll address it later). That's not to say those things aren't important. They are. But if concern for those factors rises—if you see an increasing number of employees asking about raises or grousing that a competitor has a better benefits package, for example—that might be a sign that your brand is no longer communicating a purpose or set of values that resonates with them. When that happens, you need to revisit your EVP.

- **Cynicism.** Cynicism is cancer to any organization. It starts small, spreads quickly, and can be deadly. Employees grow cynical when they become convinced that the organization cannot be trusted to keep its promises. For instance, you'll hear them complaining that a new management initiative is "more of the same." This is a Brand Contract emergency and needs to be addressed ASAP.
- **Fear of change.** As we said earlier, a consistent, strong brand and culture give employees a sense of safety that keeps them feeling confident, even when the organization is changing. If your people are exhibiting a greater fear of change—even positive changes like expansion or advancement opportunities—then you may have a problem with your Brand Contract.

PREVENTING BRAND DAMAGE

The Brand Contract is the bedrock of the EX. The stronger, clearer, and more consistent your brand message is to your employees, the better their expectations will align and the more deeply they will trust the organization. However, once the brand is damaged and trust is broken, it's extremely hard, and sometimes impossible, to repair. Better to prevent damage before it occurs by monitoring and managing your Brand Contract from both ends: what your employees perceive and what management is telling them.

Impacted by branding and other social pressures, our brains take into account a range of input—often more than logical evidence and data—when they invent, create, and evaluate our experiences.

Start with mindfulness. Simply being mindful and aware that you *have* a Brand Contract and that it's important is a great place to begin. Know your EVP. Make sure you and everyone else in your organization's leadership is aware of how their actions and the decisions of the organization impact what employees believe they have been promised. As Meghan M. Biro writes in *Forbes*:

> Make sure the stories align well and accurately reflect your current brand and the overall mission. Then look at the employee

EGGHEAD ALERT!

The Pepsi Paradox

Coca-Cola lovers may be dismayed to learn that Pepsi continually beats Coke in blind taste tests (and Pepsi isn't afraid to tout the results). Yet studies show people prefer Coke over Pepsi when they're told what they're drinking.

Brain imaging studies have found that an area of the brain called the ventromedial prefrontal cortex (VMPC) may be the culprit. In these studies, both normal people and patients with VMPC damage preferred Pepsi to Coke when they didn't know what they were drinking. But those without damage to the VMPC switched their stated preference from Pepsi to Coke when they knew what they were drinking. Those with damage to the VMPC did not.[7]

> experience—what employees do every day, the actions they take, and how they perceive the actions of their managers and top management.[8]

Next, communicate. Talk with your people at every level often and candidly. Ask them how they feel about their leaders and the direction of the organization. Do they feel that they are being treated respectfully and told the truth? What do they expect from their experience, and how does their EX line up with those expectations? Try to get a peek through their lenses. Be as straight with employees as you can about finances, possible layoffs, changes in policy, or anything else that might make them feel uneasy or that the organization has gone back on its word.

George Bernard Shaw said, "The single biggest problem in communication is the illusion that it has taken place." If your goal is to keep the Brand Contract working for you, not against you, make communication constant, clear, and two way.

Finally, question your personal values, priorities, and actions as they relate to those of the organization or department. Are they in line with what you tell your employees and customers? Are your decisions, and those of the organization, being driven by the values that the majority of your people care about, or are you doing one thing and professing to believe another? The kind of employees who will make your organization successful are also the kind of employees who care that their employer is moral, ethical, and operates according to a set of unchanging values.

If you are wavering in your values, or if there are no clear values behind the things your organization's leaders say and do, it's time to get clarity. You cannot and will not have a Brand Contract that leads to a positive, empowering EX until you know what you stand for, from the CEO's office down to the loading dock or retail storefront.

CHAPTER 5. THE BRAND CONTRACT: THE CHAPTER EXPERIENCE

- Your Brand Contract is all the implied promises that your brand identity—what you profess to be and what you stand for as an organization—makes to the people who are exposed to it.
- Your culture, marketing, reputation, media coverage, and the behavior of your people create expectations for the future, and impacts the Brand Contract.
- Through things like media coverage and the Internet, the Brand Contract actually can affect expectations of people before they come to work for you.
- Your Brand Contract plays a major role in your ability to attract talent to your organization or team.
- The Employee Value Proposition (EVP) is the value an employee receives from an organization in exchange for the employee's work.
- Your Brand Contract is an organizational weather vane created by your reputation, how your organization communicates, the values it claims to follow, the personas of your leaders, your culture, the firm's authenticity, and its level of openness.
- The Brand Contract is a tool for fostering employee engagement and loyalty. The stronger it is, the more loyal your people will be.
- This Contract shapes the Employee Experience (EX) by providing a sense of consistency, predictability, and safety in the face of continual organizational change.
- You have a strong Brand Contract when employees invest in your culture, defend the organization against detractors, feel comfortable questioning and challenging authority, and are comfortable taking risks.
- Recruitment problems, lower engagement scores, increased employee focus on pay and perks, cynicism, and fear of change are warning signs that your Brand Contract is hurting.
- Preventing Brand Contract damage is far better than repairing it after it happens.

CHAPTER 6

The Transactional Contract

> Leadership experts and the public alike extol the virtues of transformational leaders—those who set out bold objectives and take risks to change the world. We tend to downplay transactional leaders, whose goals are more modest, as mere managers.
>
> —Joseph Nye, political scientist and Harvard professor

This quote could have easily been written about grocery store chain ALDI, and we are confident that ALDI's managers would agree. ALDI executives and managers are some of the best transactional leaders we have observed, and that has been a key factor in the company's success.

That's because ALDI is a limited-assortment grocer with thin margins. For that reason, there is simply no room for misunderstanding in the ALDI culture. In the United States, ALDI operates a chain of 1,400 outlets, but across the world, the German parent entity owns and operates thousands more. When you combine all of its various holdings, ALDI is one of the largest grocery store chains in the world.

Most ALDI stores follow the same spare, efficient business model. The majority of the products carried are private label, stores are efficiently laid out, prices are lower than those of competitors, and simplicity and quality reign supreme. When you shop at ALDI, the customer's Brand Contract is absolutely clear. ALDI will generally stock what you are looking for, but the selections to choose from will be limited. The store's footprint will be easy to navigate and learn. The process of shopping for groceries will be simplified, and you can be certain you are paying the lowest price possible for quality products. In exchange for the best prices and high quality, you give up the chance to select among an endless variety of products. For some, it's a match made in heaven, a classic contract where both parties get exactly what they want with no surprises. This approach has given ALDI a loyal customer following . . . and a committed employee base.

ALDI's Employee Value Proposition (EVP) and Employee Experience (EX) reflect the same transactional efficiency. Because ALDI executives operate in a world where margins are razor thin, they have learned to create value through details and accuracy. ALDI is all about clarity and efficiency while maintaining quality. The company is masterful at establishing the Transactional Contract with employees and turning aligned expectations into a key currency that permeates the company culture.

ALDI values its employees, and treats them well. Positions throughout the company pay industry-leading wages, and the company invests heavily in the growth and development of its people. ALDI district managers are provided a lucrative compensation package, put through an extensive training program, and given responsibility for a multi-million-dollar district. Included in their rewards package is a fully expensed AUDI A3 (remember, it's a company with German roots) and an iPhone.

If you are a potential new hire scrolling through ALDI's website, you will notice that ALDI establishes its Transactional Contract right along with its Brand Contract: "The District Manager position at ALDI is a challenging one," states the first sentence of its district manager careers site.[1]

Employees are expected to take on heavy workloads, and managers are expected to assume tremendous responsibility. Managers must be flexible to various roles and assignments. ALDI employees who are willing to work hard take care of the customer, and follow procedural protocol and operating standards, thrive. This Contract puts ALDI in a position to compete favorably with other global grocery titans, while providing a desirable EX for employees that find ALDI's culture in line with their own values.

WHAT IS THE TRANSACTIONAL CONTRACT?

As subtle and ephemeral as the effects of the Brand Contract can be, the Transactional Contract is concrete and intentional. ALDI demonstrates that the Transactional Contract is a powerful, if often overlooked, tool for organizations whose goal is to establish and grow a deliberate EX based on a specific, strategic vision.

The Transactional Contract is the mutually accepted, reciprocal, and explicit agreement between two or more entities that defines the basic operating terms of the relationship. It's often codified in a document (or documents), though it doesn't have to be; Transactional Contracts can be verbal. These are *quid pro quo* contracts: something for something. *You work these hours and do this job, and we'll compensate you fairly for your work.* It's a transaction.

The Transactional Contract is the mutually accepted, reciprocal, and explicit agreement between two or more parties that defines the basic operating terms of the relationship.

Two factors make the Transactional Contract unique and important. First, it is forward-looking and anticipatory. An organization offers a prospective employee a Transactional Contract as a condition of employment and, in doing so, sets expectations for the future. It is the officially marked starting point for Expectation Alignment (EA). Sure, as we've said, expectations start forming as soon as a recruit is exposed to your brand, but you may not have control over those expectations, and they're difficult, if not impossible in most cases, to assess. The transactional process, however, starts when the person signs an employment contract accepts its terms, and comes on board.

Second, the Transactional Contract is the only one of the three subcontracts that should be fully intentional and fully explicit. It's not composed of inadvertent brand messages, psychological signals, or expectations created to fill a vacuum. It's all about terms, conditions, requirements, and rewards. Management can custom-engineer it to shape the EX in any way it chooses, and it can present the explicit terms of employment to the recruit in precise language that leaves no room for misinterpretation.

Amazon's Brand Contract begins sifting potential stars from those who won't cut it before they even apply for openings, but its Transactional Contract also sets expectations right up front. There's little confusion about what some new hires are getting themselves into: long hours and difficult workloads, but big potential rewards in fulfilling careers. What makes good Transactional Contracts (and there are bad ones, which we'll get to) work is that they are voluntary. Nobody is coercing you (though, in a difficult job market, you could argue that just being offered a job opportunity might feel coercive).

That voluntary exchange allows Amazon to get away with requiring warehouse workers who labor for a few bucks over minimum wage to sign a noncompete agreement:

> During employment and for 18 months after the Separation Date, Employee will not, directly or indirectly, whether on Employee's own behalf or on behalf of any other entity (for example, as an employee, agent, partner, or consultant), engage in or support the development, manufacture, marketing, or sale of any product or service that competes or is intended to compete with any product or service sold, offered, or otherwise provided by Amazon (or intended to be sold, offered, or otherwise provided by Amazon in the future) that Employee worked on or supported, or about which Employee obtained or received Confidential Information.[2]

Hey, you know what they say: Nice guys don't dominate the world of ecommerce.

AN OVERLOOKED WORKHORSE

The Transactional Contract is a workhorse that's often overlooked by leaders because it seems like an unglamorous legal or process obligation, the organizational development equivalent of a Toyota Camry. But it's an essential tool for shaping expectations and defining the EX. This Contract confines and structures expectations, limiting them to short-term exchanges and specific cases: "If X happens, then Y happens." It is critical to anticipating and aligning expectations.

Despite the common belief that employees always crave a free-wheeling, anything-goes workplace, they actually value structure and predictability. They might also want opportunity and an enjoyable workplace culture, but they want those things in the context of a consistent structure where surprises are kept to a minimum.

It's important to note that Transactional Contracts do not have to begin with a "whereas" and end with a signature on a dotted line. Transactional Contracts can include oral histories, well-loved slogans, employee handbooks, instruction manuals, policy guidelines, SharePoint pages, Slack channels, an internal knowledge base, and on and on.

ALDI is a good example of this. The ALDI Management System (AMS), provides a clear structure in which ALDI managers operate. The AMS is a written compilation of operating procedures that dictates what managers will do in situations that range from hiring to providing feedback to the way the store operates. Many of the company's managers refer to the AMS as their bible, and some carry with them worn, well-loved copies.

Much like a key and time signature for a jazz musician, the AMS gives ALDI managers their boundaries. As is the case with jazz, without structure, the result is chaos and disharmony. However, an accomplished jazz musician playing within the rules can fly off on a solo with full freedom to create a masterpiece while staying safely within the bounds of the larger structure.

Not a jazz fan? Even today's rap artists observe structure, such as tempo and beat. Similarly, ALDI managers are given a clear structure, but within those bounds, they have a good deal of latitude to operate as they see fit and according to their talents. Like the Brand Contract, the Transactional Contract can lend a sense of order and control to the chaos and fluidity that's the normal state of any organization.

"But doesn't that limit autonomy and creativity?" you might ask. We thought so too, until we interviewed hundreds of ALDI managers. To our surprise, rather than finding the AMS limiting, these managers found it refreshing and freeing. Rather than worrying about how to address various situations that constantly came up and consumed both time and thought, the AMS clearly spelled out what to do. This freed managers to focus on higher-level responsibilities, such as engaging employees and customers.

Picture your favorite sport, but picture it without rules or boundaries. There is no defined playing area, no regulations about whether you can throw a left hook at your opponent, and no set playing time, and there are only limited rules on what's acceptable in terms of behavior. It doesn't really matter what ball we use—basketball, football, table tennis ball, rugby ball, marbles . . . it's all the same. Oh, and there's no scorecard, even though we say we are playing to win. But it doesn't really matter anyway, because there is no agreed-on goal. In this environment, of course, there is no need for officials—why have officials when there are no rules and no objectives?

The game would be chaos, and after a few minutes of running around in all directions, the players would either be injured or bored. The Transactional Contract solves that problem. It creates structure by setting the rules and objectives of the engagement or initiative. In written or verbal form, the Transactional Contract explicitly states the terms of a broad range of workplace issues, from policy to expectations:

- Compensation and benefits
- Objectives and performance criteria
- Mutual expectations
- Vacation time
- The proper framework for performance management
- The preferred approach to customer service
- How to approach and honor company guarantees and warranties
- Nature of the job (work hours, specific responsibilities, etc.)
- Terms of employment
- How people are treated by and within the organization
- Ownership of intellectual property and noncompetition
- Confidentiality
- Policies and procedures

That's just a start. The Transactional Contract doesn't just outline legal and procedural possibilities, it defines the basic operating terms of the relationship.

"Our leaders appreciate the AMS because it empowers them in their daily roles," says David Behm, President of ALDI Inc. "The AMS distinctly outlines one's job role, areas that they are responsible for, areas that they are not responsible for, and their communication and reporting structure. There is no uncertainty about who is responsible and what is expected. This gives our management the confidence to act and lead in their areas, knowing that they have the support of their leaders. It also fosters quick decision-making, which is important in a competitive business environment."[3]

If you do this, then we'll do that. Boring stuff . . . unless you use it deliberately and creatively to shape the kind of organization you want. True, things like goals and objectives may not be written in an initial employment contract, but again, the Transactional Contract isn't limited to what's on paper. It's also made up of the ideas and concepts discussed and agreed on before and after the employment contract is offered, as well as throughout the relationship.

"The ALDI Management System was developed to provide our employees with transparency into our organizational structure, communications channels, employee responsibilities and most importantly, our governing philosophies of leadership," says Behm. "The management system was written for all employees, whether or not they have leadership responsibilities, and benefits everyone in the organization by making clear our rules of behavior and communication. We believe it fosters a cooperative leadership style in the company. The system is simple, but clearly outlines our company objectives and how our employees are empowered to achieve our goals."

WRITTEN AND VERBAL CONTRACTS

There are two types of Transactional Contracts: *written* and *verbal*. Some organizations shy away from putting many written agreements in place because they restrict employee autonomy or tie the organization down. Other organizations simply don't have their acts together, relying on improvisation without structure.

We don't recommend a cavalier approach here. A signed piece of paper or an electronic document stating that the employee understands, accepts, and agrees to adhere to such things as sexual harassment policies and confidentiality rules is essential to any organization. Certainly, an employee handbook represents an important part of the Transactional Contract. Beyond that, in practical terms, many Transactional Contracts are expressed verbally, generally through explicit statements: "We will never ask you to work weekends," or "You will be expected to hit these sales targets over the next quarter."

(In many cases, the law may also consider implied statements to be part of an employment contract, but since those are made up of the employer's past actions, statements, and treatment of other employees, they fall under our definition of the Brand Contract.)

All forms of Transactional Contracts, written or verbal, are efforts to minimize misinterpretation. Ensuring clarity is in everyone's interest. The employer wants to avoid legal liability, potential misunderstanding and gaps, and internal conflict, while the employee wants to know what is promised and expected. Because the Transactional Contract consists of a clear set of employer promises, it is the necessary starting point for all employee expectations to come.

ALDI's approach to setting expectations and communicating responsibilities engenders an internal clarity of mission that's to every stakeholder's advantage. "We conducted a companywide survey this year, and there was a question that asks, 'I understand how my work contributes to the success of ALDI.' Ninety-seven percent responded positively to that statement," says David Rinaldo, Division Vice President of the company's Haines City, Florida, division. When you have that dynamic—where you have an organization of 25,000-plus people who are well-compensated and very clearly understand what they do on a day-to-day basis as it relates to the business, our customers, and co-workers—you create something special. It allows us to operate in an organizational and operational efficiency and effectiveness that is one of our key competitive advantages."

> The Transactional Contract is an overlooked workhorse because it seems like an unglamorous legal obligation. But that misses its potential as a tool for shaping expectations and defining the EX.

TRANSACTIONAL DOESN'T MEAN SOULLESS

Despite its importance, one of the knocks against the Transactional Contract is that, if not designed correctly, it turns what should be an engaged, meaningful, trusting employer-employee relationship into, well, a *transaction.* A passage from *Personnel Psychology and Human Resources Management* nicely summarizes this belief:

> Economic pressures have created a workplace characterized by transactional forms of dealing. This, it is argued, will fashion a calculating, self-interested and opportunistic workforce, working within the "limits" of the contract and no more, in return for high compensation or remuneration.[4]

The flaw in this thinking is that the Transactional, Brand, and Psychological Contracts are mutually exclusive—that only one can govern an organization at a given time. We argue the opposite: All three are in effect at all times in any organization, running side by side, each affecting the others but governing what evolutionary biologist Stephen Jay Gould called "nonoverlapping magisteria."

Transactional Contracts are like traffic cops: They keep order and keep things moving. Employees might be on the way to doing incredible things, feeling engaged and happy because their psychological expectations are being met, but that doesn't eliminate the need for order: *This is what I will be paid, this is how many weeks of vacation I get, and this is what I'm expected to accomplish over the next six months.*

When you view organizations as collectives of employee expectations, it's clear that each Contract governs a different realm. Feelings of connection, purpose, belonging, and the organization "having my back" might be the purview of the Psychological Contract, but those feelings easily coexist with the more mundane provisions of the Transactional Contract.

When people perform work, whether they are touring with a musical group or attending to medical needs in Africa, they do so because they receive something in return—a transaction. Sometimes that reciprocal arrangement satisfies their inner need to contribute to the world. Sometimes it boils down to a paycheck. Acknowledging that and giving transactional issues the respect they deserve doesn't, in and of itself, make a workplace a soulless paycheck mill. It merely reflects the reality that in order to let employees be creative and productive, every organization also needs its procedural and legal socks pulled up and shoes tied. We've seen what happens when organizations ignore that requirement—we're looking at you, Zappos.

INTENTION AND INTERPRETATION

Apart from its power as a symbol of structure and consistency, one of the key traits of the Transactional Contract is that it's protective. It is designed to preserve and protect the fundamental, basic interests of both parties as well as to preserve the basic working relationship between them. It's there to reduce the risk of Expectation Alignment Dysfunction (EAD). Every Transactional Contract has a goal: to keep employees satisfied by ensuring them that the basic promises made throughout their employment will be kept while meeting the needs of the organization. To break it down simply:

Honoring the Transactional Contract = Satisfaction

Breaching the Transactional Contract = Dissatisfaction

But as you're aware, no Contract is as simple as words written or spoken. In order to achieve satisfaction, the parties involved in the Transactional Contract have to honor its *spirit*, not just its words.

Consider this case: In 2014, the Texas Supreme Court ruled that a group of sixty-three former DuPont employees could not proceed with their $23 million fraud lawsuit against the giant company. The employees claimed that DuPont leaders had lied when they convinced them to change jobs and move to a subsidiary, insisting that there were no plans to sell the subsidiary.

Sure enough, the employees were right. A short time later, DuPont sold the subsidiary to Koch Industries. Koch reduced salaries, benefits, and retirement account contributions, just as the employees had feared. The high court ruled that because the employees were technically covered by a collective bargaining agreement, they could not sue for fraud because the agreement provided for alternative forms of relief for termination without "just cause."[5]

The complexities of labor law are irrelevant to this discussion. What is relevant is that while DuPont honored the technical letter of its Transactional Contract, the company did not honor its spirit. Not only did DuPont wind up in a lawsuit, it now has the legacy that no union organization will ever trust the company again. The labor community is small, and memories are long.

So the success or failure of the Transactional Contract lies in the execution and in the intentions of both employer and employee. Everybody must leave the table not only with a clear understanding but an honest intention to honor the terms of the agreement and not to try to circumvent them at the first opportunity.

No Contract is as simple as words written or spoken. To achieve satisfaction, the parties involved in the Transactional Contract have to honor its spirit, not just its words. The Transactional Contract is the starting point for building trust within an organization.

The Transactional Contract is . . .

- **Promissory.** It's built on an exchange of promises or commitments. For example, the employer promises to pay a certain wage, give the employee a certain position, and offer a package of benefits and perks.

The employee promises to perform his or her duties and abide by the rules set down by HR, the boss, established law, and commonly accepted workplace standards.

- **Reciprocal and bilateral.** The Transactional Contract comes with mutual expectations that each party must meet on an ongoing basis. The employer must continue to provide the employee with a paycheck, benefits, and a safe work environment, and in return the employee must continue to show up, follow the rules, and perform as expected. The Contract is also based on a system of balances that constantly readjust. For example, if an employee consistently performs superlatively, the Contract might imply that management should (but is not obligated to) consider promotion, an increase in compensation, or both.
- **Compliance focused.** One of the main reasons for the provisions of any agreement is to provide guidance should one or both parties breach it. Contract law rests on the presumption that somewhere along the line, something in an agreement will go amiss, and there must be guidelines in place to deal with that eventuality. The Transactional Contract exists in part as a compliance tool, with possible breaches closely monitored by both sides.
- **The default setting.** The Transactional Contract represents square one. It's the North Star of an organization, the one reliable fixed point in space in a squall of relative motion and changing relationships. When there's disagreement or confusion about expectations, rules, or what was promised, all parties go back to the Transactional Contract. It's the source of the relationship and the final arbiter. Depending on the organization, there can still be room for renegotiation or compromise, but everything begins with all parties going back to the original terms.
- **Inclusive, and intended to bind parties together through mutual interests.** Both sides in any agreement want something. In an employment agreement, the employer wants someone to perform a task competently and fit into the existing culture; the employee wants fair compensation and decent working conditions. The Transactional Contract is designed to ensure compliance by meeting both sides' desires to a reasonable degree. It also includes specific provisions that address wants and needs. For instance, the employer wants the employee to adhere to a code of conduct as it relates to customer

service, so the written or verbal Contract includes that code. The employee wants opportunities for promotion, so the verbal Contract might include the employer saying "After each performance review, depending on the outcome, you may be eligible to pursue new opportunities within the organization." Each side is the other's incentive: The employer wants a productive employee; the employee wants to keep having a job.

- **Emphasizes procedural fairness and equality.** The Transactional Contract is also the rulebook for each employee's experience. Should there be a breach on either side, the Contract describes how it will be handled and ensures both parties that the outcome will be the result of a fair, equitable process. For example, a dispute over overtime will be handled through the HR department; a harassment claim made by one employee against another will be dealt with according to rigid policies intended to ensure confidentiality and fairness. Great success in resolving patient concerns results in a financial reward for hitting monthly "I care" targets. Again, everything is predictable, not left to chance.
- **Focused on tangible factors.** Because the Transactional Contract is a satisfaction tool, it deals in factors that create satisfaction but not engagement. We know from our research and engagement survey database that things like pay, perks, and benefits don't necessarily make employees feel engaged in the long-run—but they definitely can hurt engagement when they're absent. The Transactional Contract creates a "ground state" for engagement and a positive EX by ensuring that tangible basic needs—compensation, holidays, legal recourse in case of disputes, physical work environment, performance descriptors, and so on—are taken care of.
- **Can cover all transactions or a single situation.** The Transactional Contract isn't just the conditions agreed to at the outset of employment; individual events and circumstances within an organization can have their own short-term Transactional Contracts. For example, not long after Steve Jobs's return to the helm of Apple, the company began working on some revolutionary new products. The company had been bedeviled by leaks in the past, so management let everyone know that the work was to be kept in the strictest confidence. However, the company also monitored employee emails and found that four employees had sent out emails detailing the new products under development.

Those employees were immediately terminated, and there were no further leaks.[6] The warning against leaks that accompanied those new projects was its own stand-alone Transactional Contract. It did not supersede the larger Contract each Apple employee had agreed to; instead, it addressed a specific situation that was unforeseeable when the original Contract was written.

- **Identifies breaches.** The Contract creates safety by giving everyone clarity regarding what constitutes a violation of its terms, so everybody knows where they stand. The short-term Transactional Contract established by Jobs and Apple in the last example identified a breach with absolute clarity: You leaked, you were in violation.
- **Is renegotiated only through mutual agreement, and formal changes are required.** One of the most valuable aspects of the Transactional Contract (assuming all parties deal in good faith) is that it can't be discarded on a whim. Once both parties agree to it, the Contract has the weight of law (or policy); changing any provision requires both parties to consent to a redraft and opens the entire agreement up to renegotiation. That tends to make everyone involved cautious about asking for frivolous changes.
- **Values conformity above creativity.** Even in the most disruptive, creative, risk-friendly organizations, some degree of conformity is essential. Employees and management alike need to adhere to some code of conduct, strive to reach commonly accepted goals, and represent the brand according to a consistent set of values. The alternative is every-man-for-himself chaos. The nature of the Transactional Contract enforces reasonable conformity by requiring everyone to play by the same rules. Variations and exceptions are up to the various players.

SUPPORTING THE TRANSACTIONAL CONTRACT

One of the most interesting aspects of the Transactional Contract is that the Brand and Psychological Contracts are critical to its effectiveness. The utility of the Transactional Contract hinges on both parties being willing to abide by the terms they've agreed to. But employees and employers both violate those terms all the time: sharing secrets, reneging on promises, giving raises or bonuses outside of compensation agreements, you name it. While a Transactional Contract often can bend slightly before it breaks (and many employees and organizations are masters at manipulating the Contract), it can take only so much. Like a bank account, taking more out of the transactional account than is available isn't a viable long-term strategy; overdraft can carry a relationship only for so long, and at a heavy price.

Having strong Brand and Psychological Contracts in an organization makes everyone less likely to breach the Transactional Contract. Why? Because while the Transactional Contract addresses hygiene factors, the other contracts align expectations, help employees engage, and create a terrific EX. Employees become happy, invested, passionate people who really care about doing great work; they don't violate the Transactional Contract because they don't want to mess up a good thing. Because engaged employees often become high achievers and leaders, managers of the organization are discouraged from violating the Transactional Contract, as well. They don't want to lose good people!

The three subcontracts work together, synergistically, to create a healthier organization where all needs—emotional, financial, motivational, and even spiritual—are met for everyone.

EGGHEAD ALERT!

Motivation-Hygiene Theory

American psychologist Frederick Herzberg's motivation-hygiene theory proposes that people are influenced by two factors: those that impact motivation and basic "hygiene factors" that influence job satisfaction. Motivation factors include things like challenging work, growth, recognition, and responsibility. Hygiene factors consist of pay and benefits, working conditions, and job security (among others). Herzberg suggests that while the presence of hygiene factors does not create motivation, the lack of them creates demotivation. For example, while an individual may not be motivated by a physically safe workplace (when was the last time you woke up excited to get to work because you knew you wouldn't be mugged that day?), not having that safety would cause severe demotivation.

RED FLAGS

Michael Nesmith, of the musical group The Monkees, once said, "The only people who steal are thieves, and that's a very small percentage of civilization. Most people want to have some way to make the economic transaction valid. They want to return the favor, if you will . . . return the benefit and reciprocate."[7] In other words, most people want to play by the rules and be honorable, and that's certainly true in any organization. Still, there are always bad apples, and a poorly drawn Transactional Contract creates unwanted opportunities for those apples to make themselves known. It also keeps honest people honest.

These are some of the warning signs that indicate your Transactional Contract is putting you at risk (and damaging your Brand and Psychological Contracts, too):

- **Legal action.** Your Transactional Contract is a framework for legal activity, but it shouldn't *provoke* unnecessary litigation. If you find yourself in arbitration or in full-fledged lawsuits more often than other similar organizations, there may be aspects of your Transactional Contract that invite legal trouble.
- **Disputes.** When issues like performance, promotions, and leave are unclear, disputes and hurt feelings are certainties. Even legal battles can arise. Make sure everything in your written and verbal contracts is spelled out in painstaking detail.
- **Irrational expectations.** As we saw when discussing EA, employees will put up with a challenging work environment if they expect it going in. If your people have all manner of unrealistic expectations—from stock options and profit sharing to promotions and international travel—your Transactional Contract may be creating those expectations or leaving enough gray area that employees' imaginations are free to roam.
- **Rule breaking.** Clear rules (and clear sanctions for breaking them) are essential for an orderly, egalitarian workplace. They're also essential for performance. If your people are constantly violating the rules, or continually underperforming to your or the organization's expectations, it may be that your Transactional Contract doesn't make them clear enough. Or perhaps it indicates no Contract is in place.

- **Difficulty letting go.** Part of the Transactional Contract should spell out the conditions and process under which someone, or the contract itself, can be terminated. That's critical, since you don't want bad actors sabotaging your organization. If holding people accountable is difficult, it's highly possible that your Contract isn't clear. If dismissing an employee is difficult and costly, or if you shy away from it because you worry that it will be difficult and costly, perhaps your Transactional Contract needs to be revised.
- **Declining Performance.** The Transactional Contract is where performance expectations are clearly outlined. If performance is declining, or not at acceptable standards, it may be because expectations are not aligned, or simply not understood. A solid Transactional Contract spells out performance expectations for both employee and employer.

> The Transactional Contract is the North Star of an organization, the one reliable fixed point in space in a sea of relative motion and changing relationships.

TAKING NOTHING FOR GRANTED

The single biggest reason that organizations get tripped up by their Transactional Contracts is that they treat them as boilerplate that doesn't need a lot of attention. Nothing could be further from the truth. In fact, we find that in many cases where people are underperforming, it can be directly tied to a poor Transactional Contract (or one that was never put in place at all).

The Transactional Contract is the foundation of employee satisfaction, and unless satisfaction factors are in line, engagement will not happen. So, while amending your Brand Contract is a big-picture problem that requires a cultural transformation and some soul searching, if you want to change your EX, start with your Transactional Contract.

A bulletproof Transactional Contract starts with attention to the details in your written employment contract and any other written materials (such as policy manuals, performance expectations, job descriptions, etc.) you give to employees or prospective hires. What kinds of expectations are you establishing with these documents? Are they realistic and sustainable? Are you clearly communicating expectations, rules, policies, opportunities, and penalties? Are these things fair and reasonable? Do they contribute to the wants and desires of both sides? Most important, how could you revise your Contract to encourage an EX that results in the kind of organization you want?

Now look at your verbal Contract. What do you or your HR team say to interviewees or new hires? Do you overpromise? What are your managers saying about future possibilities, such as advancement and compensation? Do you rely on verbal exchanges to deal with issues that should be set down in writing? When you speak to employees about what to expect, are you clear and realistic? What have you, as a manager, communicated to your team? Are you aligned in those expectations?

Finally, take a look at how you and the organization have handled the Transactional Contract in the past. Do you approach the terms fairly, or have you been inconsistent? How have you dealt with employees who violate the Contract? What is the organization's reputation for fairness and equity in dealing with things like pay and benefits? Are you known for keeping your promises or not? Do you reinforce the Contract as it relates to performance, or do you let that side of the equation slip by, without consequences or actions?

IT'S NOT JUST ABOUT LAWS AND RULES

Before we move on, we want to be sure we haven't given you the wrong impression. The Transactional Contract isn't always made up of legalese and HR policy. And it's not just about what is cooked up at corporate HQ.

Let's go back to your new hire, Olivia, who joined your firm back in Chapter 5. Olivia did her research on the company, found a clear connection with your EVP, and accepted your employment offer. Since that time, she has really shone, leading the customer advocacy department in customer complaint resolution success. She's a keeper.

When Olivia joined, she was told that there weren't enough offices, so she'd have a temporary desk just to the side of reception for the time being, until an office became available. But that hasn't happened yet, and nearly six months have passed. Still, she's managed to hold up her end of the contract, and her superior ratings attest to that fact. Further, her supervisor let her know that they were still working on the bonus plan, which would be based on performance, and that Olivia would be eligible to participate once they nailed it down. Six months later, great ratings, no bonus plan. The boss just hasn't had time to get around to it.

No legal documents were signed. Technically, no explicit verbal agreements were made. But even though no dates were set, promises were made—enough that a sensible person like Olivia would form some reasonable expectations. After all, the spirit of the Transactional Contract should also be honored. But those expectations have not been met in Olivia's mind.

Let's take a look at Olivia's case through the organizational lens, the employee lens, and the leader lens.

Speaking for the organization and seeing things through the organization's viewpoint, you have every intention of honoring the transactional agreement. You fully intend to move Olivia into an office, as well as give her the financial performance bonus she deserves, once you are able to do so. But you've had clients occupying the extra office for the past four months (they were supposed to be finished several months ago), and you can't kick them out until their business is finished next month. Also, the division is finally ready to roll out the new compensation and reward plan, but you actually have a promotion opportunity for Olivia in leading the smart parts assembly division. However, you believe she needs to gain additional financial understanding. You're sure she will be thrilled but haven't been able to offer the promotion to her until all of the cogs are in motion. Besides, this makes the office issue moot, because she'll be down on the assembly floor.

Peering through the employee lens, Olivia sees things differently. She believes she has been an excellent employee, has met all expectations (and beyond), but that she's not getting back what she's put into the Contract. While she wasn't actually promised she would move into an office within a short time period, the commitment was explicit enough, and she doesn't understand why it is taking so long. It's a big building, and the company could surely move her in if they really wanted to. It's not so much the office itself but that promises weren't kept. She knows she could use additional knowledge of finance, but it's certainly not needed in her current role, so that couldn't be the holdup. Between this and not getting her bonus, she's asking friends about job opportunities elsewhere. She loves the company but doesn't want to work where she's not appreciated and where commitments aren't kept.

The leader lens reveals the bigger picture. True, the organization made some promises. It's also true that the organization intends to keep those promises as soon as it can. At the same time, Olivia is feeling abandoned, since nobody is taking the time to explain what is going on. Further, she may not be aware that, while she is performing well, she is missing some financial skills that would require a simple investment of time to acquire. It doesn't really matter who is wrong or right here. The organization is about to lose a very valuable employee. The situation needs to be taken care of, and quickly.

Taking the time to see the Transactional Contract through the leader lens will greatly reduce Expectation Alignment Dysfunction (EAD). Without doing so, however, both the organization and the employee are left to invent their own realities.

Effective Transactional Contracts will enhance your organization by freeing everyone from worrying about minutiae and technicalities so they can use their energy innovating, serving customers, and growing (just ask our friends at ALDI). These Contracts are anticipatory; they show a path forward. They will also eliminate EAD. So, ask yourself: "Would either party, employer or employee, be unclear on the terms of our Transactional Contract?" This isn't a one-time query. This question must be asked over and over again. Pay attention to the details, take nothing for granted, and treat this contract as what it is: an essential tool for EA.

CHAPTER 6. THE TRANSACTIONAL CONTRACT: THE CHAPTER EXPERIENCE

- The Transactional Contract is the mutually accepted, reciprocal, and explicit agreement between two or more entities that defines the basic operating terms of the relationship.
- Employee performance problems are often caused by an unclear, misaligned, or missing Transactional Contract.
- It is the only contract that's fully intentional, making it a critical component in EA.
- Though the Transactional Contract can seem dull or rote, it's actually the bulwark of the EX because it adds structure and predictability to offset the potential chaos of the Brand and Psychological Contracts.
- The Transactional Contract is a tool for creating satisfaction, but not necessarily engagement.
- Transactional Contracts can be written or verbal, but they are always explicit.
- Transactional Contracts don't make an organization soulless or focus its people only on compensation. Instead, they lend structure to employee expectations and the EX.
- The Brand and Psychological Contracts make the Transactional Contract more effective by fostering engagement and a positive EX, which in turn make employees and employers less likely to violate the terms of the Transactional Contract.
- Warning signs that your Transactional Contract is not working well are disputes, regular legal battles, irrational expectations, constant breaking of the rules, poor performance, and difficulty holding employees accountable.
- To ensure that your Transactional Contract is an asset, don't treat it as boilerplate. Instead, review it carefully through the leader lens, taking nothing for granted.

CHAPTER 7

The Psychological Contract

> There is nothing either good or bad, but thinking makes it so.
>
> —William Shakespeare, *Hamlet*, Act 2, Scene 2

The Brand Contract and the Transactional Contract address employee expectations that are typically evident and open. They are intentional and purposeful. However, other expectations are often veiled and obscure. Consider our earlier analogy that a Contract is like an iceberg. The visible part above the water is the Brand Contract *and* the Transactional Contract. The mass lurking below the waterline, hidden from view, is the Psychological Contract. These are the expectations in a relationship that remain largely unstated and implied. The following story illustrates what we mean.

We were discussing with a close friend the differences between two prominent CEOs. Both had built technology companies worth hundreds of millions of dollars. Our friend had worked closely with both leaders, and a question arose: What was the biggest difference between them? The surprising answer had to do with the simple act of walking.

On one occasion, our friend had been walking in New York City with one of the CEOs and his team. As the group walked, the executive unconsciously lined his people up according to rank, with the next most important person in the company walking next to him and the subordinates following behind according to their perceived place in the organization.

Later, our friend found himself in a similar situation in San Francisco, observing the second CEO as the group walked to dinner. But this time, as the entourage began walking, some of them started to hang back. The CEO stopped and invited all members of the group to catch up, stay close, and walk with him, not behind him.

Two similar stories, two completely different Psychological Contracts. It's not hard to see why both CEOs were respected, but one was beloved.

LEADERSHIP AND THE PSYCHOLOGICAL CONTRACT

The Psychological Contract has been placed last in our rubric because, while the Brand Contract and the Transactional Contract are essential, the Psychological Contract has the greatest potential influence on the Employee Experience (EX). Hidden in our hearts are the ideas, hopes, and dreams that truly define us. These expectations cannot be addressed adequately by clauses in an employment contract or hiring slogans that attempt to align expectations. These expectations are part of the Psychological Contract. The Psychological Contract is the unwritten, implicit set of expectations and obligations that define the terms of exchange in a relationship. Transformational leaders know this and use the Psychological Contract to tap into the enormous power sealed in these expectations.

The Psychological Contract is the unwritten, implicit set of expectations and obligations that define the terms of exchange in a relationship.

When President Franklin Roosevelt took office in 1933, the Great Depression was destroying the United States' economy along with the American people's will to fight. Unemployment stood at 25 percent—even higher in some parts of the country. Nearly one-fifth of the nation's farms had been sold. Bank withdrawals were restricted out of fear that a run by cash-desperate account holders would cause the system to collapse. Leaders worried that the nation's social fabric was close to deteriorating into anarchy and violence. By 1933, economic carnage ravaged the country's GDP, which fell by half from 1929 to 1933.[1]

Roosevelt stepped into the crosshairs of the worst economic crisis in modern history and immediately began looking for solutions. With no specific ideas in place at his inauguration, he leaned on his "Brain Trust," an informal group of advisors. Together with cabinet officials, members of this think tank began cobbling together a plan to save the nation. It included such revolutionary (for the time) concepts as a forty-hour workweek, a minimum wage, Social Security, universal health insurance, workers' compensation, unemployment compensation, and laws banning child labor, most of which have become entrenched throughout the world today.

In 1933 and 1934, FDR exercised executive power in a way that has never been seen in the United States before or since, creating dozens of new government agencies: the Works Project Administration, the Resettlement Administration, the Civilian Conservation Corps, the Agricultural Adjustment Administration, and many others. The staggeringly large program, which Roosevelt called "a new deal for the American people," was built on what came to be known as the "Three Rs":

1. **Relief.** Measures designed to temporarily employ and aid millions of impoverished families, elderly people, children, and those with disabilities.
2. **Recovery.** Measures designed to stop the bleeding and spark new economic growth, including price supports and stimulating industrial production.
3. **Reform.** Measures designed to prevent another catastrophe, including the creation of the Federal Deposit Insurance Corporation and the Securities and Exchange Commission.

Yet the economy wasn't the only thing suffering; the American people were suffering, too, and not just physically. The Great Depression was inflicting deep psychological wounds. Rather than fomenting revolution as many plutocrats feared, Americans were actually frightened, depressed, and hopeless, beaten down by the endless privations of daily life.

Roosevelt and his advisors understood that their "New Deal" needed to address these psychological wounds just as much as it needed to help Americans find work. From this perspective, the New Deal was far more than a politician's plan to get America back on track. It was a Psychological Contract with the American people. The New Deal told them that someone was in charge and that their leaders were going to restore some semblance of the good life that had been taken from them.

We could write a thousand-page book on the New Deal alone, particularly viewing it as a Psychological Contract between the government and the governed. But it suffices to say that the program not only revived the U.S. economy between 1933 and 1937, it also gave hope to the American people.

FDR's New Deal wasn't just an economic contract. It wasn't just about jobs and saving farms. It was about motivating a downtrodden people. It was a Psychological Contract of hope.

SOMEONE'S IN CHARGE

Some regarded FDR as poorly qualified to be president when he took office, and he may have been. But he exhibited something critical to guiding the wounded nation through the worst economic storm in its history: a clear understanding of the people's need for trust and confidence in their government.

In his First Inaugural Address on March 4, 1933, he said, "Confidence . . . thrives on honesty, on honor, on the sacredness of obligations, on faithful protection and on unselfish performance. Without them it cannot live."[2] Regardless of whether you agree with Roosevelt's political leanings, the New Deal and this view of confidence, obligations, and performance were important to all citizens because it said to the American people, "Someone's in charge. We're going to survive this. There's a plan. If you're down and hurting, we're going to help you get back up."

That promise created emotional stability that allowed the massive economic angst to die down long enough for other programs to restore farm prices, imports, and industrial activity. The New Deal wasn't perfect, of course. But so what? Even if the American people didn't get fair value for the bridges, hospitals, national park overlooks, and parkways that were built, so what? They got stability.

People began to believe that FDR was in charge—that the country wasn't in free fall anymore. The contract created the expectation that if Americans didn't panic, left their money in the banks and the stock market, and worked hard, everything would be all right. It was transformational. FDR's vision for the American people illustrates the *power* and the *purpose* of the Psychological Contract.

MATTERS OF THE HEART CAN BE HARD

With the Psychological Contract, the leader's challenge lies in understanding and managing something that is dependent on elements such as feelings, perceptions, culture, memories, and other cognitive dynamics. These factors cannot always be easily defined or measured. Your organization may have a compelling Employee Value Proposition, a great reputation (Brand Contract) and a drawer full of pristine employee documentation (Transactional Contract), but without accounting for the Psychological Contract, you don't know if the messages are complete or if the expectations are aligned.

The Psychological Contract is something that anyone who has been part of an organization could identify—an "I can't describe it, but I know it when I see it" sort of phenomenon. Observing the Psychological Contract can be like looking for a black hole in astrophysics: Sometimes you can define it only by what's not there.

Faced with such murkiness, you might be tempted to ignore the Psychological Contract as being too nebulous to worry about. That would be a mistake. Even though you may be unable to point to the Psychological Contract within your organization or your relationships, you can't ignore it. Remember the iceberg and what happened when Captain Smith ignored ice warnings on the *Titanic*'s maiden voyage.

POWERED BY EXPECTATIONS

Let's look first at a modern example of the Psychological Contract in action—social entrepreneurship.

Microfinance is the practice of providing loans and other financial services to low-income people who have no access to traditional banking. Economics professor and Nobel laureate Dr. Mohammad Yunus popularized modern microfinance in the 1970s, and since that time it has attracted investors, spawned Internet startups, and grown exponentially. According to *Microfinance Barometer 2014*, 91.4 million people around the globe received $81.5 billion in microloans to start businesses, run farms, purchase livestock, and buy necessary technology ranging from mobile phones to water pumps and solar cells.[3]

But what makes microfinance even more interesting to us is the fact that the Psychological Contract makes it possible. Not the Transactional Contract; that's typically a standard loan agreement specifying the amount of money to be borrowed and the terms of repayment. No, what's fascinating is the psychological agreement that exists between lender and borrower, binding the two parties together.

Sixty-eight percent of microfinance borrowers are women.[4] Why? Because men of the villages have proven to be more likely to squander the money, much of it on vices like excessive drinking. (We decline to comment on what that says about the male gender.) Women have proven more responsible, and that's led to some extraordinary repayment rates. For instance, online microlending network Kiva reports that 98.42 percent of its more than 1 million loans have been repaid.

In part, that's the result of a *psychological* agreement between investors and borrowers that says, "We trust you and believe in you, so we are willing to lend you funds where nobody else will." A microloan to an impoverished mother of six in Uganda is a show of faith and respect, and the resulting pride is what makes microfinance so effectively self-enforcing. No one wants to break a contract that brings with it such a powerful sense of self-worth, and that's a big reason why so many women entrepreneurs (and, to be fair, some men, as well) have turned loans of $50 and $500 into new freedom from poverty. Where a normal Transactional Contract would collapse (there really isn't much a microfinance lender can do to enforce the transactional agreement), the expectations established by both the New Deal in the 1930s and modern microloan finance illustrate the power of the Psychological Contract.

STUDYING THE PSYCHOLOGICAL CONTRACT

Let's say a division of a company has a new employee join its team. The new recruit, Ésme, found her dream job through an online posting. She was impressed by what the ad referred to as a "fast-paced, innovative culture where people with ideas can thrive." As the company is one of the largest and most respected employers in the area, it's not surprising that she has known of it for a number of years. In fact, her aunt was a longtime employee of the company until she retired last year. The company's reputation (Brand Contract) is definitely solid, and two of Ésme's friends who now work for the company gush about their jobs.

Before Ésme even starts her first day of work, she is contacted by the hiring manager, the general manager, and her immediate boss, welcoming her on board. Each explains the expectations of her role, and these expectations are emphasized again during her new-hire orientation.

Ésme is especially glad to hear that what her friends have told her about the company's working environment and benefits are accurate (generous paid time off policy, flexibility, fair compensation, opportunity to participate in training programs, etc.). It appears the Transactional Contract is all in order. Thumbs up.

Ésme, as with all of her colleagues (and each of us, for that matter), expects to be treated with dignity and respect. She expects to be listened to and that she will be cared about as a person, not just as another employee. She takes these expectations for granted, and assumes they will be part of the working relationship.

Ésme hopes this company will be a place where she can plant herself for a while. She plans on giving her all and knows she has a lot to offer. It's a great job; she will be a great employee, at least in her mind. One of the reasons she was excited to join the company was that she wants to have an impact. She wants her ideas to be taken into consideration and wants the opportunity to make a difference—and she knows she can. She doesn't want a job where she puts in her eight hours and then doesn't think about it for the rest of the evening. She is committed to the company and hopes that the organization is equally committed to her.

Where is all that stated in the Contract? Where does it say "Ésme, part of your job is to make a difference in the world, and we will pay you for it"? There may be a hint of it in the Brand Contact, as on the surface the company appears to be innovative and to value fresh ideas. It even claims to be a strong supporter of the community, which is appealing. But it's not spelled out anywhere. It's not in the Transactional Contract, either. It's part of the *Psychological* Contract.

The notion of the Psychological Contract has been around since the early 1960s, when Harvard Business School professor and management theorist Chris Argyris first referred to the "psychological work contract." During that time, unionization and collective bargaining agreements were prevalent, due largely to the need to improve working conditions, which were sometimes less than ideal.

Prior to this era, work often required little thinking and reflected ways of working that had been around for centuries. Even most office jobs were designed such that employees followed procedures, but weren't expected to bring innovation or creative problem-solving to their roles. Employees did their jobs and got paid. The most valuable aspect of the Brand Contract was stability: Employees wanted jobs they could keep for a long time, maybe even retire from.

Frederick Taylor, the father of scientific management theory and the assembly-line mentality, referred to this sort of corporate culture as "pick up a pig and walk," meaning your job was to do what the boss told you to do. There was no talk of employee expectations, dreams, goals, innovation, or needs. Taylor said of managers, "When he tells you to pick up a pig and walk, you pick it up and walk, and when he tells you to sit down and rest, you sit down. You do that right through the day. And what's more, no backtalk."[5] That was the Contract. It wasn't pretty, but it was certainly clear.

Argyris observed, however, that employees aren't machines. They have ideas, opinions, beliefs, family, background experiences, and other factors that shape the way they view their employment. They form expectations of their employment situation, and their performance reflects whether those expectations have been met or not.

After observing the relationship between foremen and crews, Argyris noted:

> Since the foremen realize the employees in this system will tend to produce optimally under passive leadership, and since the employees agree, a relationship may be hypothesized to evolve between the employees and the foremen which might be called the "psychological work contract."[6]

These observations marked an important shift in the employer-employee relationship. Following on the heels of Argyris, MIT professor Edgar Schein observed that both individuals and organizations have expectations (sounds vaguely familiar, doesn't it?). Together, those expectations form a Psychological Contract. Each side has a set of expectations for the other side that aren't part of any written agreement, but they directly impact behavior. On the organizational side, the Contract is backed by authority. By joining the organization, an employee accepts the authority of the organization. On the employee side, the employee can influence the organization, based on his or her expectations, in order to protect his or her interests and desires.

While Argyris and Schein argued that the Psychological Contract contains an implied agreement regarding expectations, Carnegie Mellon professor Denise Rousseau claimed that the two parties don't have to agree in order for the Psychological Contract to exist. One party doesn't even have to know the other has expectations, and the perceived contract can still exist. Thus Rousseau defined the Psychological Contract as "an individual's belief that a promise has been made and a consideration offered in exchange for it, binding the parties to some sort of reciprocal obligations."[7]

Some contend that the term "Psychological Contract" is a misnomer, as it has little to do with the way the mind functions (the "psychology" piece). Further, they argue, without mutual agreement, there cannot be a contract. While no single definition exists, the Psychological Contract is something, as stated earlier, that most of us can recognize—especially when it is not working the way it should.

CREATED, INTERPRETED, EXAMINED, ACTED UPON

Despite arguments to the contrary, we find the term very appropriate. The Psychological Contract gets its name because the human mind is where it is created, interpreted, examined, and acted upon—and it certainly creates an understanding in one's mind that there is an agreement:

Created. The Psychological Contract doesn't exist on a piece of paper or in a policy manual. It's not born to a marketing campaign. It's created within the minds of each party, often separately and without common agreement.

Interpreted. Although two employees may face identical employment circumstances, they may each interpret the Contract differently based on factors ranging from personal background to religious beliefs. An organization will interpret the Contract through the organizational lens, while an employee interprets it through the employee lens.

Examined. A Transactional Contract is subject to the scrutiny of HR, supervisors, employees, and even the legal system. Similarly, the Brand Contract is a public contract, available for all to examine. The Psychological Contract, however, is checked privately, within one's own mind.

Acted Upon. Our behavior is directly impacted by our perception of the degree to which our Psychological Contract is honored. However, the outcome isn't always apparent. The outcome might be a change in perception, a shift in emotion, or a difference in engagement.

MOM'S ON THE ROOF

There's an old joke (a pretty bad one, in fact) that goes something like this: Larry goes out of town for a week and asks his brother to take care of his favorite cat. After an enjoyable week on the beach, he phones his brother to see when it might be convenient to drop by and pick up his cat. His brother stumbles for a moment, then blurts out, "The cat's dead!" and hangs up the phone without another word.

Devastated, Larry calls back and confirms that, indeed, his cat is dead. Larry shouts at his brother for his perceived lack of sympathy for something that was obviously so important to Larry. His brother apologizes, saying "I'm sorry, the cat died a few days ago and I didn't know how to break the news to you."

Larry explains, "You could have at least eased me into it so I wouldn't be so shocked. When I called the other day you could have told me the cat was on the roof and wouldn't come down. Then maybe the next time you could have told me the cat fell off the roof and that he was at the vet. At least you could have prepared me. Then it might have been easier to hear that the poor cat had died."

Frustrated, Larry attempts to end the conversation. However, his brother stops Larry before he can hang up, saying "Uh . . . by the way, Mom is on the roof and won't come down."

This humorous anecdote is the perfect setup for some compelling research findings. Recent studies looked at organizations that went through downsizing and found that these layoffs severely damaged morale and engagement. In addition to confirming the existence of common sense (it's tough to be engaged when coworkers on both sides of you are clearing out their cubicles), these studies found some other interesting points. Not only did the organization lose the people who were let go, the number of employees who left the organization after downsizing initiatives was actually *five times* the number laid off.[8]

The layoffs were a violation of the Psychological Contract, and the attrition was the damage. While a Brand or Transactional Contract will never say "We guarantee your long-term employment"—organizations go to great lengths *not* to imply this—for employees of these companies, the Psychological Contract suggested they were valued. When the kiss-of-death announcements were made, employees immediately rewrote their Psychological Contracts to anticipate the next chapter: *We can't trust you and you'll let more of us go without warning.* Preservation mode kicked in, and they looked for new employment elsewhere. With the Psychological Contract violated, the Brand and Transactional Contracts weren't worth the paper they weren't printed on.

WHAT FORMS THE PSYCHOLOGICAL CONTRACT

The Psychological Contact has some unique qualities that set it apart from the other two Contacts. The Psychological Contract is:

- **Implicit.** The terms and intended outcomes of the Psychological Contract might be discussed, but often are not.
- **Unilateral**. The terms are not always mutually agreed upon or even understood by both sides. Each party forms its own terms and expectations.
- **Left to interpretation.** As the terms are often unilateral, interpretation often differs between parties. Violation of the Contract is largely perceptual and can easily go unnoticed by the other party.
- **Belief based.** The Psychological Contract is based on each side's *beliefs* about mutual obligations. In other words, what matters is what each side believes both parties are expected to do, not the agreed-upon requirements.
- **Nonreciprocal.** Unlike the Transactional Contact, with Psychological Contracts there is no *quid pro quo* exchange. Not every component of one side's Contract must correspond to an action on the other side.
- **About fairness.** Both parties pay attention to the fairness of the *process* rather than to just the fairness of outcomes. "How" is just as important as "what."
- **Open-ended and dynamic.** The Psychological Contract doesn't seek to tie down all potential outcomes or possibilities, because it can't. It is constantly being rewritten and evolves based on the state of one or both parties.
- **Flexible.** The Psychological Contract can withstand short-term violations if the long-term investment is perceived to be worthwhile. Further, the Contract is looked at as a whole, rather than as a set of individual elements, so even if parts are violated, the larger Contract can still remain healthy.
- **Illogical.** The Psychological Contract is emotional and based on perception, bias, and emotion.
- **Inclusive.** The Psychological Contract takes over when the others are AWOL.

That last point is particularly important. Every relationship has a Contract. In the absence of a clear Brand Contract or a comprehensive Transactional Contract, the Psychological Contract takes over. Humans aren't very good with information vacuums, so if no Contract exists, we'll create one in our minds. It is this characteristic that gives the Psychological Contract its power. In the end, it will always have a seat at the table because it applies even in the absence of explicit terms and conditions.

> In the absence of a clear Brand Contract and a comprehensive Transactional Contract, the Psychological Contract takes over.

DON'T WAIT UNTIL IT'S TOO LATE

Consider this scenario. A new senior-level employee is brought onboard a small technology firm. The firm has only been around for thirteen months, so it is still in growth and startup mode. The employee works his rear end off for the first six months because he knows that although he isn't being paid well (in fact, he actually didn't get a paycheck last month), it's what's necessary to take the business to the next level. And it's starting to pay off, as the company looks like it will finally have its first profitable quarter.

Sure enough, the company makes a profit, and the employee is given not only his missed paycheck but a 10 percent bonus. Fantastic! The next step, which is to discuss ownership and equity in the company, is obvious in the employee's mind.

But when he brings up his terms with the owner, the owner is taken by surprise. Nobody ever talked about giving up ownership! Whoops. An Expectation Gap the size of the Grand Canyon just opened up.

Both sides set expectations. Those expectations turned into Psychological Contracts. Though it was never discussed, the Brand Contract implied that as a technology startup—an inherently risky environment where employees often give their all for minimal pay with the hope of stock option gold at the end of the rainbow—equity would be on the table. The employer assumed the "minimal pay" part was true; the employee focused on the equity part.

The Transactional Contract consisted of a non-compete agreement, a discussion of compensation, and an outdated policy manual copied from a previous employer. There were no clear guidelines for performance or rewards.

Brain, meet vacuum. Without express promises, both parties created their own set of expectations—Psychological Contracts. For the employee, this meant "work hard and get ownership." For the employer, it meant "hire a good professional, reward him with bonuses when we become profitable, and grow my company." What's also unsaid is that the boss, the founder, has sacrificed everything, including his life savings and his marriage, to make a go of this company. He's not about to surrender even a sliver of equity. Lack of awareness of the Psychological Contract leads to a breach that's more perceived than real, but it's damaging nonetheless.

PSYCHOLOGY AND THE EMPLOYEE EXPERIENCE

When the Psychological Contract is breached (we'll talk more about this in the next chapter), the result is often psychological (and even physical) disengagement in the relationship. In the case of our new employee, this could mean anything from a refusal to continue putting in long hours to resignation and a lawsuit.

Remember the study earlier in this chapter where employees quit their organizations after layoffs were announced? Most didn't leave because they were part of a reduction in headcount; they chose to leave because in their minds, the organization had violated their trust unforgivably.

In looking at our own attrition research data, our team found not only similar results, but also something potentially more damaging. Often, employees who leave an organization of their own volition after downsizing are also those who are valuable enough that they have little trouble finding work elsewhere. That's why they can afford to leave over a perceived trust violation.

Employees who stick around after downsizing are usually the dedicated employees (who are, of course, still valuable) and the less employable workers who can't get hired elsewhere. So when an organization obliterates the Psychological Contract with a thoughtless action, it also chases away many of their most skilled, engaged people—the ones who made the company successful in the first place. What often remains is a top layer of dedicated employees over a body of unemployable people whose mere presence sows seeds of discontent.

The Psychological Contract—and its fulfillment or violation—is a critical factor in the EX. It has a profound effect on engagement. What employers failed to recognize over the centuries—and many still don't even today—is that the Psychological Contract plays a major role in whether employees choose to give their hearts, spirits, minds, and hands to their work. In fact, studies show that fulfillment of the Psychological Contract can predict half (49.9 percent) of the variance in employee engagement.[9]

Honoring the Psychological Contract = Engagement

Violating the Psychological Contract = Disengagement

Our beliefs and our expectations are reference points against which we compare our EX. That EX depends on the degree to which expectations and perceived obligations—the substance of the Psychological Contract—are fulfilled. Depending on whether they are and how, we will reaffirm our perceptions and have a positive EX, change our beliefs when discrepancies exist, or exit the relationship.

Whether in the workplace or in life, when the Psychological Contract is honored, we engage in that relationship. When the contract is violated, we disengage.

AN ALIEN CONCEPT

In 1954, social psychologist Leon Festinger and his associates came across newspaper reports surrounding a religious group whose members were preparing for the end of the world. A woman from Chicago founded the group after she claimed to have received "messages from the planet Clarion." These messages outlined the destruction of the world through a great flood that was to take place before dawn on December 21, 1954. The woman, later known as Sister Thedra, managed to win the faith and support of a number of followers whose expectations aligned with her predictions.

Convinced of their beliefs, the group made drastic preparations for the apocalypse. They gave away their possessions, left their jobs and families, and gathered in preparation.

According to the followers, a UFO would arrive at their gathering place prior to the flood and grant them safe passage to the planet

Clarion in time to escape the disaster. An expectation was set, and group members placed their confidence not only in the event coming to pass but in their leader, as well. A Psychological Contract was formed. Faithful members of the group, who did what they believed was expected of them, would escape the catastrophic event.

The commitment of this group intrigued Festinger and his colleagues. They were even more fascinated by what would happen to the group's zeal when the time for the cataclysm came and went without event. When the appointed hour passed without the arrival of a UFO or a flood, the reaction of the group members was interesting. Some, as predicted, left the group, seeing that what they had come to expect was a falsehood. Their contract had been violated.

However, others increased their proselyting efforts. Their convictions actually became *stronger*. According to the group, because they had "spread so much light, God had saved the world from destruction."

This second group made for an interesting study. In what Festinger refers to as a "disconfirmation of belief," a conflict was created between their perceived reality and the actual events. They eliminated the conflict by discounting the events that took place—rather, the events that did *not* take place—and shifted "reality." They created a new Contract.[10]

MAKING SENSE OF THE CONTRACT

Humans are wired to resolve cognitive dissonance and changing beliefs and expectations however we can. We don't do well with conflicting Contracts. Just as the ear wants to hear dissonant music resolve, it's the natural desire of both individuals and organizations to resolve dissonance.

We all have a tendency to believe the world is as we see it—that our view is correct. We form expectations, both of ourselves and of others, to support that view. When confronted with evidence to the contrary, we attempt to reduce this conflict by justifying, blaming, or denying, among other things. Less often, we see the disconnect in beliefs for what it is, and look for ways out. That's why disagreements over politics and religion are usually intractable; they are about worldviews, which change grudgingly, if at all.

EGGHEAD ALERT!

Cognitive Dissonance

When an internal psychological conflict is the result of two contradictory or incongruous beliefs or attitudes, it is known as cognitive dissonance. Dissonance also occurs when an individual is confronted with new information that is at odds with current beliefs or values. As we value internal consistency (consonance), when we experience dissonance, we become psychologically uncomfortable, and we try to reduce this conflict.

If a man smokes, for example, but believes that smoking is bad for his health, he may experience dissonance. He can reduce this dissonance by changing his behavior (quit smoking) or by changing his cognition through shifting his own beliefs about whether smoking is actually unhealthy.

Our minds aren't good with unresolved dissonance. We try to resolve confusion and lack of clarity by searching for cues from our environment and interpreting their meaning. When confronted with lack of clarity or ambiguity, or when we feel our expectations haven't been met, we try to make sense of what is going on around us. We interpret the cues—actions by the organization, interactions with others, conversations with the boss, memos, and the like—in ways that create meaning. We try to make sense of what's going on in a process that organizational theorists call *sensemaking*.[11] Really, that's what it's called.

It's important to understand sensemaking because it helps us see how Psychological Contracts form. Where information is ambiguous or lacking, we try to fill in the blanks. Sometimes this is logical. Other times we invent our own reality or story based on our needs and identity: "The boss never brings me in on critical projects, therefore she must not trust me, which means I had better look for another job." We interpret the Contract for ourselves, which is perilous.

If employer and employee don't clarify the missing pieces of the puzzle, each side will form its own Psychological Contract and set of expectations. For this reason, understanding and clarifying the content of the Psychological Contracts of both employer and employee is essential.

TIME FOR A CONTRACT REVISION

Let's take another look at CHG Healthcare, the company we mentioned earlier in the book. If you remember, CHG was a good company, but not good enough in a competitive industry where there was little differentiation between players. CHG wanted to be great. In order to do so, the organization realized it had to address all three Contracts—in some cases making expectations clear, in others establishing a new Contract.

CHG realigned and clarified its internal and external Brand Contracts around "Putting People First." The concept became a way to describe not just how CHG did business, but who it was. This concept meant that everyone would need to start thinking differently about the value of people. Additionally, by putting into place accountability systems, clear job descriptions, and more precise performance expectations, CHG realigned the Transactional Contract. This took time, and change didn't happen overnight.

Perhaps the most difficult Contract to realign, however, was the Psychological Contract. Employees had formed expectations and beliefs about their roles and work. Some employees, including some executives, could not comprehend the shift in the message to "We're not going in the right direction, we need to change course, and your jobs are about to change." Some resigned while others were encouraged to leave.

To make this shift in thinking and behavior work, CHG had to reestablish and clarify expectations for its leaders and its employees. Unlike those waiting for the ship to Clarion, however, the leaders of the organization weren't asking people to follow along blindly. They let employees know the old Contract was null and void. The leaders set new expectations for the company that said: "We will not be the same company as before. This isn't just about what we do, it's about who we are. If you're on board with that, great. If you're not, we wish you well."

"This [change] starts with the intention to build a company that you're proud of, in the same way that you're proud of your family or the way that you conduct yourself," said CHG CEO Scott Beck. "You're trustworthy, you take care of each other, you have each other's backs, you learn from mistakes, and you all help each other reach your potential. Those are the things we aspire to achieve in our personal lives, so there's no reason not to bring them to the corporate environment, too."[12]

ALIGNING THE PSYCHOLOGICAL CONTRACT

Aligning the expectations created by the Psychological Contract is not for the faint of heart. It's subjective, relies on perceptions, is illogical, changes often, and is based on many different variables and perspectives. But it *can* be done; just ask CHG.

Start by nailing down your Brand and Transactional Contracts. As we said, the Psychological Contract fills in the blanks left by the other two Contracts. If it's not clear in one of the other Contracts, human nature is to assume the Psychological Contract rules.

Then have important conversations. Ask questions. Strong leaders listen and then defuse explosive situations simply by asking good questions and acting on the answers. Does an employee expect rapid development? Informal mentorship from the CEO? The ability to interact with high-level clients? Power and prestige? The most up-to-date software apps? Such expectations may not always be rational, but they matter.

Finally, match the Psychological Contract to your organization's mission. All CHG employees know that their Contract involves putting people first. It permeates all they do. Be clear about your own Psychological Contract. Help employees understand the "why" behind the "what." When you do so, you'll stop being seen as automatons running a business and start being seen as people working together for a common cause.

CHAPTER 7. THE PSYCHOLOGICAL CONTRACT: THE CHAPTER EXPERIENCE

- Although Brand and Transactional Contracts are the most visible parts of Contracts, like an iceberg, the Psychological Contract makes up the bulk of your Contract.
- The Psychological Contract is the unwritten, implicit set of expectations and obligations that define the terms of exchange in a relationship.
- The Psychological Contract is powered by expectations.
- The Psychological Contract is created, interpreted, examined, and acted upon in the mind.
- Unlike the Brand and Transactional Contracts, the Psychological Contract is implied and often illogical.
- When we feel the Psychological Contract is honored, we engage. When it is violated, we disengage.
- In the absence of a clear Brand Contract and a comprehensive Transactional Contract, the Psychological Contract takes over.
- When our view is ambiguous or unclear, or when our expectations are not met, we use sensemaking to interpret, assign meaning to, and act upon the cues in front of us.

Trust

CHAPTER 8

Moments of Truth

Learning to trust is one of life's most difficult tasks.

—Isaac Watts, English theologian

On November 23, 2014, Abdo Ghazi, a San Francisco–based driver for the controversial ride-hailing company Uber, was the victim of a frightening assault when a passenger allegedly jumped into the front seat of his car, punched him, and stabbed him in the face. Ghazi, who suffered a broken nose and puncture wounds, wound up missing two months of work—not only as an Uber driver, but also from his day job as a custodian. So on April 28, 2015, he filed suit against Uber for workers' compensation.[1]

If you pay attention to tech or business news, you already know that Uber doesn't always have the most sterling reputation when it comes to relationships. The high-flying Silicon Valley "unicorn" has been accused of trying to strong-arm municipal governments into changing taxi regulations and generally behaving in a high-handed, entitled manner. So you might suspect that under the circumstances, an organization that has gained this sort of reputation, whether accurate or not, might go out of its way to behave humanely when a serious injury to an employee puts it under the microscope, right?

From its beginnings, Uber has insisted that its drivers are independent contractors and therefore not entitled to benefits or workers' compensation protection. The company refused to back down from that stance in Ghazi's case. Uber's legal team filed a motion to take the case to arbitration and outside of the workers' compensation system, a motion the presiding judge denied. At this writing, the proceedings were on hold pending Uber's appeal of the decision.[2]

For contrast, let's look at Airbnb again. In March 2014, a Manhattan host rented his apartment via the home-sharing service, only to find that it had been used for a destructive, very public, all-night party. How did Airbnb respond to this embarrassingly well-publicized event? Like

Uber, it could have claimed that the risk of loss was entirely on the host. Instead, Airbnb quickly and decisively stepped in and handled the matter on behalf of the property owner.

Airbnb had dealt with past guest transgressions and furious property owners, including a 2011 incident in which a renter basically destroyed a host's apartment and Airbnb dithered over whether it would offer compensation. Not eager to repeat that embarrassment, the company had a plan in place by the time the Manhattan overnight bacchanalia lit up social networks. Within 24 hours, Airbnb had sent the host to a hotel for a week, sent a locksmith to his apartment to change the locks, and wired him $23,817 to pay for repairs and cleanup.[3]

Both incidents and their aftermaths epitomize "moments of truth," or MOTs. In a moment of truth, the Contract that both employer and employee have established is put to the test. Until a MOT occurs, any Contract—the Brand piece with its implied promises, the Transactional piece with its explicit promises, and the Psychological piece with its messy web of expectations and beliefs—is theoretical and untested.

But once a MOT arrives, the Contract gets very real. Employees quickly learn whether their employers or supervisors will keep their promises. They also find out in stark terms how the organization's leaders view them, which can be a pleasant surprise or a rude awakening.

MOTS AND THE CONTRACT

What kind of shape do you think Uber's Contract with its drivers was in after it refused to explore workers' comp for the injured Abdo Ghazi? Factor in ongoing lawsuits claiming that the company's position on drivers as contractors is unlawful and it's a safe bet its Contract is murky, at best. This might be one reason the company is losing market share to rivals Lyft and Via.[4]

In contrast, Airbnb's quick action to take care of its most valuable asset—its hosts—has garnered the company a great deal of goodwill and positive press coverage. The company still has its detractors, especially local governments that lose out on hotel occupancy taxes when visitors stay in an Airbnb property, but overall the company has a positive image and a seemingly strong Contract with its hosts. Meanwhile, Uber has developed a reputation in some minds as being indifferent to the welfare of the people behind the wheel who make its staggering $60 billion valuation possible.

When something happens that tests the validity of the promises that make up the Contract, that's a moment of truth. Also, from the employee's perspective, it doesn't really matter as much whether the outcome of the MOT is positive or negative, as long as the outcome is consistent with expectations.

Every moment of truth is also a potential turbulence point in the Expectation Gap, that space between what employees expect and what they experience. Think of MOTs as the bumpers in a pinball machine.

FIGURE 8.1 MOTs deflecting Expectation Alignment

Depending on the position of MOTs, expectations can ricochet off them in virtually any direction.

When MOTs contradict the express promises made in the Transactional Contract or the implied promises of the Brand Contract, there's turbulence. Non-fulfillment of the Contract deflects expectations hither and yon as employees worry, become angry and feel betrayed, or simply disengage.

That's a dysfunctional organization or team. Mismanagement of moments of truth has created a situation where no one trusts anyone else. It's an adversarial, ugly, every-person-for-himself environment where service and performance are likely in steep decline along with profits. The Customer Experience (CX) goes right off the cliff along with the EX.

When something happens that tests the validity of the promises that make up the Contract, that's a moment of truth.

REINFORCE, VIOLATE, CREATE

The result of a collision between expectations and MOTs is like what happens when physicists at the Large Hadron Collider bring elementary particles together at near-light velocities: unpredictable energies and particles hurtling off on random vectors. Those energies and particles can be harnessed for greater productivity, or they can rampage out of control and destroy the entire system.

What's essential for leaders at all levels to understand is that MOTs are never neutral. They *always* have an impact. In fact, a MOT always has one of the three effects we discussed in the Contract section:

1. **It reinforces the Contract.** Suppose a private university positioned as an ethical, progressive employer informs a new hire during the orientation process that should an employee become pregnant while working there, she will receive up to three months of paid maternity leave. Two months into her employment, the new hire finds out that she's expecting. After she leaves to give birth, the university not only follows through on that promise but sends a tech to her home to set her up with a portable home office, so she can work if she chooses to. That's delivering on expectations, increasing trust,

and reinforcing the belief that at the next MOT, the organization will come through.

2. **It violates the Contract.** What if, after the woman has her baby, the university says, "We've changed that policy. Under the new rules, you don't get the three months of paid leave until you've worked here for three years." The employee feels that her employer has lied to her and broken her trust. Or, alternatively, someone failed to align expectations from the beginning and did not inform the employee of the three-year employment requirement. Either way, the Contract has been violated, and she's going to be much less likely to trust the university to do right by her in the future unless some serious damage repair takes place.
3. **It generates a new Contract.** What if, instead of returning to her position after maternity leave, our university staffer is presented with the option to be a full-time telecommuter and work from home? She can be home with her baby and quit making a long commute . . . but new things will be expected of her. She'll have to attend regular online meetings, fill in an online time sheet, and, of course, adapt to juggling her work demands with the needs of caring for her child. If she accepts, then a new Contract has been created. The old one isn't necessarily torn up; some of the expectations she formed upon being hired still might stand. But this new Contract is definitely dominant.

This triangle of reinforce, contradict, or create isn't limited to MOTs. Every day, things happen within any organization that support, contradict, or change employee expectations. Even if they don't realize it, employees always have their leaders on trial, watching to see whether they honor the spirit of the Contract and care about expectations. The way in which leaders handle expectations on a daily basis determines the Employee Experience.

This doesn't mean you should worry that changing from metal to plastic utensils in the break room will cripple employee morale. Not everything is a crisis. However, it does mean that it pays to be mindful and intentional about decisions that could have a negative effect on EA and the EX. At the very least, before taking action of some impact, ask yourself this question: "How will the proposed action impact the Contract I have in place with my people? Will this be a moment of truth or just a blip?"

EGGHEAD ALERT!

Phantoms in the Brain

Respected neuroscientist, V.S. Ramachandran, is known for his work with those who have experienced amputation. Despite these injuries, these victims often retain all or part of the normal sensations of a functional, intact limb—pain, itching, etc. Ramachandran explains that this is because the brain has a "body image," a representation of itself that includes the missing limb. While some suggest that this perception is because the person experiences some denial that the limb is lost, he also notes that some born without limbs still experience the vivid sensation of having the use of the limb (they never had). He addresses one case where one young girl, born without arms, frequently used her "fingers" to do simple math calculations.

Ramachandran's work seems to prove Freud's theory that our brain develops mechanisms (perceptions, thoughts, behaviors) to look for (and even invent) "evidence" that supports our expectations, whether real or imagined.[5]

RUBBER, MEET ROAD

Mindfulness and intentionality haven't been at the top of the traditional inventory of leadership skills, *but they should be.* A change to the Contract, whether company-wide or between a team lead and a line employee, evokes powerful emotions that can dramatically affect your EX and engagement:

- **Reinforcement** of the Contract leads to feelings of *safety* and *validation.* Employees feel more secure and believe more strongly that they can trust in and invest themselves in the organization. They also feel good about themselves for having believed in the organization. A relationship of trust is the result.
- **Violation** produces *anger* and *cynicism.* Employees feel varying degrees of anger at the organization, ranging from annoyance to rage, for not keeping its promises. Because they also feel manipulated and

even betrayed, they can develop the cynical belief that the organization's leaders can't be relied on to do anything they say they will. It's not hard to see how this attitude can lead to total disengagement. A relationship of distrust is the result.

Incidentally, revising the Contract, even when changes are minor, is often seen as a violation. The thinking goes, if the organization can change its mind at the drop of a hat, what will change next? Even if the change in the Contract is positive, the fact that it can change suddenly, and without the employee's consent, can create a net negative outcome. Revision can lead to *uncertainty* and *worry*.

- **Creation** of a new Contract may lead not only to *confusion* but also *curiosity*. These aren't necessarily negative emotions, but confusion can lead to more problematic feelings if employees remain unsure about the new rules, their new roles, or what's expected of them. That's one of the reasons why change is hard. But communication is key. Curiosity can be a force for good and presents an opportunity to engage employees at a deeper level. Depending on the way the new Contract is handled, a relationship of trust or distrust could be the result.

These emotions are where the rubber meets the road with the Contract. They're what you have to acknowledge and manage. Your subordinates aren't going to say "You violated our Contract last week when you announced that pay freeze." But they will reveal their anger, cynicism, and feelings of betrayal in subtle ways . . . and some that aren't subtle. Being mindful of those emotions isn't a touchy-feely New Age management trope; it's a leadership survival skill.

A change to the Contract, whether company-wide or between a team lead and a line employee, often evokes powerful emotions that can dramatically affect your EX and engagement.

INDIRECT MOMENTS OF TRUTH

Just when you thought you were done with employee expectations and MOTs, there's this: You also have to deal with *indirect* moments of truth. When an individual employee reaches a MOT, the outcome of that moment sometimes can impact not only that person's emotional state and trust in the organization but other people's as well.

Take our pregnant university employee. If the university denies her the maternity leave it promised, do you think she'll keep that to herself? Probably not. She'll tell her spouse, her coworkers, her Facebook friends, everyone under the sun. She's angry, and remember, it doesn't matter if her anger is justified or not. What matters is only whether expectations have been met or violated.

A 2012 study conducted by the Sanders School of Business at the University of British Columbia backs this idea up. The researchers found that employees who witness workplace bullying were more likely to want to quit their jobs than the employees who were actually being bullied.[6] Why? Because the organization faced a moment of truth and came up short. Everyone who witnessed the violation felt that their faith had been betrayed. Such a failure may set off seismic rumblings that can tear an organization apart.

That brings up another challenge in dealing with moments of truth: They can occur without your knowledge. For example, the bullying that the Sanders School of Business researchers studied were not planned events like performance reviews; bullying was seemingly built into the culture of those organizations, like buggy code in a computer operating system. The leaders might not have even been aware of the problem until they noticed higher turnover and poor employee morale, but by then the damage would likely be difficult to reverse.

Every day, things happen within any organization that support, contradict, or change employee expectations.

CHRONOS AND KAIROS

The first step to making sense of a system as dynamic and organic as expectations and Contracts is to apply some structure to them, and that's what we've done by dividing moments of truth into two categories called *Chronos* and *Kairos*.[7]

Chronos comes from the Greek word for "time." Chronos moments, as you might imagine, are moments of truth that happen at predetermined points in the timeline of an employee's term of service with an organization. They are part of the Employee Life Cycle.

Pre-Hire and Recruiting

- The job search or the employment listing
- The job interview
- The job offer and the terms of the employment contract

Onboarding

- Orientation and induction
- Training
- Benefits overview with HR

Compensation

- Raises and bonuses
- Benefits
- Incentives

Performance

- Performance reviews
- Recognition for accomplishments
- Disciplinary action

Growth & Development

- Additional training and professional development
- New assignments
- Promotions

Exit

- Termination or layoffs
- Resignation
- Exit interview
- Post-exit

Chronos moments are inherently predictable and controllable. They're often moments of truth that leaders can plan for, times that they can anticipate how employees might respond to different possible outcomes. A perfect example is the ubiquitous annual performance review. A leader with foresight, knowing that a certain employee was going to receive a subpar review, could plan for that employee's likely response by taking proactive steps: using different language to describe the performance problems, offering suggestions and incentives for improving performance before they're asked for, and so on.

In addition, Chronos moments are largely about the Transactional Contract and the express promises it contains—compensation, bonus structure, the time frames of performance reviews, benefits, and the like. They also require sound management, but not a great deal of visionary leadership. You can remove a fair amount of the volatility and risk from Chronos moments by properly constructing your Transactional Contract, being hyperaware of expectations, and being in control of the variables for each one as much as possible—carefully constructing job postings and descriptions to avoid creating unrealistic expectations, for instance.

Unfortunately, because they seem to be merely procedural, transactional checkmarks, leaders often overlook the transformative power of Chronos events. That's a mistake. Take onboarding, for example. Many organizations think it means handing out an employee manual and holding an orientation meeting. But it can be much more.

As Red Branch Media founder Maren Hogan states in *Forbes,* her organization creates a "narrative" that begins with the job advertisement and runs through to the employee's first day on the job. She writes:

> We give them a reason to believe (we're a family business and bootstrapped so the founders work as hard as the interns) and a map to what their future could be (we tell stories of our successful employees and the highs and lows that got them there).[8]

A 2012 study published by the Academy of Management showed support in the first ninety days of employment to be one of the strongest predictors of positive later work outcomes, so organizations like Red Branch Media may be on to something.[9]

> The way in which an organization handles Chronos and Kairos moments predicts its Expectation Alignment, level of trust in leaders, Employee Engagement, and Customer Experience.

THE RIGHT MOMENT

The transformative power of Chronos moments—for good or ill—pales in comparison to that of Kairos moments, however. Kairos translates from the Greek roughly as "the right moment" and refers to MOTs that are inherently unpredictable and tend to be tied to the underlying culture and values of the organization. They're not tied to a schedule, and can't always be anticipated. Some examples:

- Customer complaints or concerns
- Conflict between colleagues
- Workplace romances
- Project failures
- Headcount reductions
- Employee lifestyle changes like childbirth, illness, or divorce
- Substance abuse
- Outside job offers
- Unusually demanding workloads

The nature of Kairos moments is that they can't be reliably predicted, so success in managing them isn't about process. It's about mindfulness, culture, and strong Expectation Alignment. Those lead to trust and a sense of safety, and that's what gets employees through when a project falls flat or a customer bucks a complaint up the chain to the top. When that happens, positive outcomes depend on employees expecting that leaders will adhere to a promised set of values, and on leaders adhering to them.

Kairos moments are really about building and reinforcing the Psychological Contract. Turning these moments into opportunities to enhance trust means addressing the Psychological Contract with intention and foresight. Leaders need to have plans in place that help employees deal with surprises, especially when they are negative ones. Leaders must also be mindful of the impact of decisions such as layoffs have on trust and expectations and have the foresight to mitigate the impact of such decisions on employee morale.

> Where Chronos events are about process, Kairos events are about culture and fabric. If your organization hasn't laid the groundwork to build trust before such events occur, there's not much you can do after the fact to create it. The damage is probably done.

IT COMES DOWN TO TRUST

Everything in this book is designed to help you foster *trust*, whether at the organizational level or the team level. Managing the Expectation Gap and creating EA allows trust to take root. Maintaining strong Contracts lets trust grow steadily. Stepping up in moments of truth makes trust lasting and resilient, and helps your organization be sustainable. Trust is the oxygen of the EX. With it, you have life. Without it, trust dies.

A trust crisis can damage even the strongest brands. In September 2015, the Environmental Protection Agency announced evidence that Volkswagen had outfitted many of its diesel cars in the United States with "cheat software" that made it appear that the vehicles were conforming to U.S. emissions standards, when in fact they were belching out forty times the allowable level of pollutants.

The company continues to face investigations by multiple national governments, class action lawsuits, and billions in possible fines. But none of this would have been possible had VW not built a culture that allowed it to happen.

Many investigators and journalists believe that the fraud was the work of a small group of upper-echelon employees acting on their own, but that many more employees knew about it. If these theories are correct, VW leadership created the expectation in some employees that unethical behavior was permissible if it served the bottom line. On the other side of the Expectation Gap, employees took that to mean "Cool! Let's violate some emissions laws!" Or something to that effect, in German.

Whatever the internal particulars, the fact remains that for years, no one stepped up to report wrongdoing. This suggests there was a belief throughout parts of the company, at least, that unethical, immoral, and even criminal behavior was to be tolerated as long as everybody looked the other way and pretended they were working for a good company that shared their values. As discussed in the *Philadelphia Business Journal*:

> Where was the board in assessing the tone at the top and culture nurtured by now former CEO [Martin] Winterkorn? What was the tone and culture nurtured by lower-level managers?[10]

A 2015 U.S. sales decline following the scandal was reversed, but from an employee perspective, "Dieselgate" was a catastrophe. CEO Winterkorn resigned. VW suspended numerous engineers and other employees, including those who were likely innocent of any wrongdoing, to prevent anyone from interfering with its internal investigation.[11]

A whistleblower sued the company over his termination.[12] More than fifty employees accepted immunity from termination in return for their testimony. Worst of all, facing massive fines and a plummeting share price, VW announced it would be cutting 30,000 jobs,[13] yet top executives—we are not making this up—say they will *not* forgo their annual bonuses.[14] Customers may get over it, at least for now, but it's likely that employee trust in the company has been shattered.

> Kairos moments are moments of truth that are inherently unpredictable and tend to be tied to the underlying culture and values of the organization.

TRUST ACCOUNTS

The Volkswagen scandal embodies a basic principle: Trust is a continuum, not a state. It is always being increased or decreased.

Trust isn't static. It can't be expected to run on autopilot. The level of trust your employees have in you today won't be the same tomorrow. Moments of truth impact trust, but so does any behavior that affects your Contracts with your people. Affirm and reinforce the Contracts and you grow trust; violate them and you cause it to wither.

Taken together, every action and decision that affects trust also affects an organization's *trust account.* We're not talking about a financial account in which a trustee controls assets for the benefit of another party. This trust account is psychological. It represents the amount of trust that the organization has earned by actions that meet employee expectations and honor the three Contracts. We call this *trust equity.* If your organization consistency upholds your Psychological Contract with your people, meets reasonable expectations, and acts according to its values at moments of truth, it will have a lot of trust equity in its account.

A high trust equity balance allows an organization's leader to do something we all do: make mistakes. Mistakes are the ultimate arbiters of the Employee Experience. They test employees' belief not only in your ethics and honesty, but also in your competency.

If you have upheld your Contracts consistently, you've been depositing enormous amounts of goodwill into your trust account. That's good, because when somebody in a leadership position makes an error, they can make a trust withdrawal without depleting the account. Because you've proven repeatedly that your intentions are honorable and you back up your stated values with action, employees are likely to cut you some slack, especially if you're honest about the mistake. A strong trust equity balance lets you make some mistakes without damaging trust.

MORE TRUST, GREATER AGILITY

Agility—the ability to adapt to shifts in the market by making rapid changes to your business model—is a prized quality in virtually any industry. In order to be agile while maintaining a sustainable workforce, you need a big balance in your trust account. Employees may say they want a creative, free-form environment, but when it comes down to it, they value creativity and spontaneity in a *reliable, predictable context* where paychecks arrive on time, everybody follows the same rules, and so on. Agility means fast changes that upend predictability, making some employees uncomfortable and harming their experience.

Let's suppose your team has been working diligently on a new product, one that was supposed to be an important part of the future of the company. Two months into your push to complete the product, your R&D team discovers the product needs to take a different turn, which will make half of the work already completed unusable. Your task as manager is to break the news to the team that much of what they've completed over the past two months simply can't be used.

Trust makes agile business practices possible by making employees more comfortable with course changes. When a company revises its strategy or adopts a completely new technology platform, it's changing its Psychological Contract with employees (and maybe its Transactional Contract, too).

Some of your employees may see the R&D shift as a violation. The degree to which employees will let you *bend* the Contract without pushback depends on how strongly they believe that the organization's interests and their interests are aligned.

That depends on the balance in your Trust Account. If you have earned people's trust with consistent behavior, transparency, and respect for your Contracts, they're apt to be flexible and roll with whatever changes you propose, as long as you eventually restore stability. They trust that you're looking out for their interests.

This dynamic applies for customers, too. Let's say you have a favorite restaurant you've been going to for years. You've come to expect terrific service, and it always delivers. Then a new owner comes in and service starts going downhill. Not completely shut-the-place-down downhill, but not at levels you had come to expect.

Because you've built up a positive balance of Trust Equity toward the restaurant, you let the service issues slide for a while. With each negative experience, that trust balance gets depleted, but until it nears zero you'll probably give the place the benefit of the doubt. That gives the place time to improve the service before losing your complete trust as a customer and losing your business. And, as many businesses have learned, often times the most loyal customers are those for whom you've corrected a service problem.

As you might expect, Chronos and Kairos moments of truth have a *major* impact on your account balance. But it's critical to appreciate that many other kinds of interactions also constitute either deposits or withdrawals from your trust account:

Interactions That Increase Trust Equity

- Caring about family
- Acts of kindness
- Listening
- Accommodating an emergency
- Recognition of achievements or longevity
- Leaders taking responsibility for mistakes
- Open, honest feedback
- Regular, productive dialogue

Interactions That Decrease Trust Equity

- Refusing to accommodate inconvenient events
- Management blaming employees for mistakes or problems
- Managers taking all the credit for a team's successes
- Inconsistent application of rules or policies
- Not showing concern for family or personal needs
- Bullying employees
- Secrecy or lack of transparency
- Irrational operational or financial decisions
- High-handed decision making without explanation

Remember, employees do not see you as just a person. You aren't simply a human being making decisions based on your good intentions and best available information. You are also the organization, or at least the face of the organization. The higher up the management food chain you are, the greater your impact on trust. A manager's unethical behavior will erode trust primarily just in her department (which is still dangerous in itself), while a CEO acting unethically could undermine trust in the entire organization, as it did with VW.

Remember, the Employee Experience, like the Customer Experience, rests on the bedrock of trust. All roads—alignment, Contracts, moments of truth—lead to trust. In the end, your job as a leader is to build deep trust that's embedded in your culture, trust that makes employees feel confident, secure, heard, and taken care of. That's what frees them to engage fully.

This trust account represents the amount of trust that the organization has earned by actions that meet employee expectations and honor the three Contracts.

ONCE MORE INTO THE BREACH, MY FRIENDS

Even the most enlightened, self-aware leaders occasionally breach employees' trust. But breaches need not be something to fear, because they often can be turned into opportunities to *increase* Trust Equity.

We're not talking about spinning something negative into something positive or manipulating the truth. Before you can fix a breach of trust, it's important to know what constitutes such a breach. We define a breach of trust as any action that clearly violates the terms of the Brand, Transactional, or Psychological Contract. For example:

- **Brand breach.** Your culture has a long-standing reputation for being welcoming to innovation, creativity, and off-the-wall ideas. But when a quirky newcomer with a flash drive full of new concepts brings them to his boss, he is shut down completely by statements like "It won't work here."
- **Transactional breach.** Your employment agreement includes a six-month paid sabbatical after ten years. But when a key employee reaches the ten-year mark and wants to take her sabbatical, sales are

down. If she wants to take the six months, you will hold her position, but you can't pay her.

- **Psychological breach.** Your employees have come to expect a robust, two-way feedback channel with management. But you're being acquired, and things in the C-suite get very busy. Anxious employees send a flood of questions, but management doesn't respond to them for weeks, leaving people confused, nervous about their employment, and angry.

Each of those breaches damages trust, but whether the damage is permanent or temporary depends on how leaders respond to repair the breach, as well as what's in the trust account. But first, understand that breaches are inevitable. You will make them, usually inadvertently, and then catch yourself and ask, "Wait, is that in the spirit of our Psychological Contract?" Those breaches generally aren't the problems. Those that go undetected and unaddressed can eat away at trust and destroy your EX. So let's look at the four factors that determine the severity of a breach.

First, there's **intention**. Was the breach due to an oversight, or was it a deliberate violation? In our own company, we've caught ourselves changing programs or direction without thinking about the impact on the Contract. In such cases, we quickly reversed course. That's an accident or oversight, and if trust is strong, employees usually won't hold such things against you. But in employees' minds, it's a different story if you knowingly break a promise.

Then there's **frequency**. How often do breaches occur? Infrequent breaches can be chalked up to distracted people doing their best in a busy environment, but when they happen all the time, employees become less forgiving.

Then there's **amplitude**. How severe are the consequences of the breach? It's one thing for the receptionist to forget to book someone in a window seat on a flight instead of the aisle. It's quite another for a company to promise its workforce there will absolutely, positively be no more layoffs and then, six months later, announce a massive workforce reduction. That kind of high-amplitude breach will annihilate trust.

Finally, there's **recovery**. What did you do to recover from the breach? Admitting responsibility and apologizing are the bare minimum, and they must be done quickly. But what else? Do you do the minimum suggested by HR and legal, or do you have empathy and make things right on a human level?

SORRY SEEMS TO BE THE HARDEST WORD

As we said, a trust breach is an opportunity to demonstrate that the Contracts you have with your people are more than paper and assumptions and to optimize EA by revealing the character of the people who are often invisible behind the company façade. If your breach was unintentional and you act quickly, apologize sincerely, accept responsibility, and take steps to ensure it doesn't happen again, often even a severe breach can *enhance* trust and increase equity.

We've found the secret: the *apology*. Apologies do much more than simply pin responsibility on someone or express remorse (though those are important, too). They imply respect for the party receiving the apology. They suggest the responsible party is mindful and empathetic. And they defuse the anger of the victims of the violation by letting them know they've been heard. Of course, those words "I'm sorry" aren't always easy to say, especially in an organizational context. As Maurice E. Schweitzer, Alison Wood Brooks, and Adam D. Galinsky wrote in the *Harvard Business Journal*:

> Apologies are even more difficult in an organizational context. When considering whether and how to apologize, even seasoned leaders can become gripped by indecision. That's understandable. A company mistake is often caused by a single division or employee, and a bad situation is frequently made worse by events beyond its control.[15]

The solution: Look at your Contracts. *All* of them. Which Contract did the breach violate? If it violated more than one, which violation was the most damaging? Start there. What was the promise expressed in that Contract, and how did your actions violate it? Knowing that, you'll know how to be specific in expressing remorse for the breach and, more important, in repairing it by taking corrective action.

We're not experts in apologies, but apart from being prompt and specific, we do know that the most important part of apologizing is being sincere. A sincere apology, even if you don't do much else, can go a long way toward repairing trust. An insincere apology will eat away at trust even if you take other corrective steps.

British Petroleum (BP) learned this the hard way in the wake of the disastrous 2010 *Deep Horizon* oil spill. Despite the billions of dollars in damage, untold devastation of local habitats and economies, and thousands of people displaced, CEO Tony Hayward committed the ultimate sin when he said to a reporter, "We're sorry for the massive disruption it's caused to their lives. There's no one who wants this thing over more than I do, I'd like my life back."[16] The statement was seen as classic clueless, self-absorbed executive privilege, and a few weeks later, Hayward resigned. Despite BP spending billions to restore the Gulf Coast areas affected by the spill, that unfortunate comment hangs over the company like a shroud.

Insincerity, appearing like you're apologizing for selfish reasons—that's the kiss of death. A good apology is about owning up and, above all, promising to make things right. At that end of the spectrum we find the Four Seasons luxury hotel chain.

A friend of ours was staying at a Four Seasons location and had requested a wake-up call so he could make an important meeting. As in many upscale hotels, at the Four Seasons, wake-up calls are not automated; a live person calls your room. But in this case, no one made the call, and the guest was late for his meeting.

How would most hotel chains respond, if they responded at all? A free orange juice, perhaps? Not at the Four Seasons. The transgression required a more personal apology. The guest was sent a gourmet breakfast that morning, and a lavish gift basket awaited him on his return along with a handwritten note of apology from the manager. It was clear that the manager on duty felt terrible about the oversight, and that sincerity salvaged the guest's experience.

What started out as a negative CX quickly turned positive—not because of an online survey but because the staff stepped up and nailed the apology. Needless to say, that wasn't the last time this particular guest stayed at a Four Seasons property. Remember, EX = CX.

> Breaches need not be something to fear, because you can actually turn them into opportunities to increase Trust Equity.

IT'S ABOUT CHARACTER

There's an old saying: "Hard times don't build character, they reveal it." Moments of truth don't just affect trust. They reveal the character of the people leading an organization. And character is what it all comes down to. Often, the people running the show are obscured by titles, perks, and the dubious glamour of being important players in their fields. It's easy to forget that they are people at all.

Moments of truth—a confrontation, a crisis, an apology—show even the most accomplished leaders as what they are: people. And we trust people when we know their character. Can they be trusted to keep their word? Do they walk their talk? Do they have the right priorities? Are they open and honest? Do they listen to criticism as well as compliments? Your MOTs reveal your character to your people.

Your Contract depends on their outcome. If you're true to your values, that connection is where the MAGIC starts and the EX shines.

CHAPTER 8. MOMENTS OF TRUTH: THE CHAPTER EXPERIENCE

- Moments of truth (MOTs) test the validity of your Brand, Transactional, and Psychological Contracts with employees.
- When MOTs support and reinforce the Contracts, expectations align. When MOTs result in broken promises, Expectation Alignment suffers.
- MOTs reinforce, violate, or create a new Contract. Reinforcement leads to feelings of safety and validation. Violation produces anger and cynicism. Even revisions can be seen as a violation and lead to uncertainty and worry. Creating a new Contract leads to confusion but also curiosity.
- MOTs come in two types: Chronos moments, which are predictable events tied to the employee life cycle; and Kairos moments, which are unpredictable events that tend to be more tied to character and culture.
- Trust manifests in the form of the Trust Account, which represents the amount of trust the organization has built up with employees by repeatedly meeting expectations and keeping the promises expressed in the Contracts.
- Trust is never static; it's a continuum and is always increasing or decreasing. MOTs that support Contracts increase Trust Equity; MOTs that break Contracts decrease it.
- Breaches of trust depend on four factors: intention (if the breach was accidental or deliberate); frequency (how often breaches happen); amplitude (how severe the breach is); and response (how the offending party makes things right).
- The key to healing a breach is the apology. Admitting a mistake and trying to fix it—quickly and sincerely—can turn even severe breaches into opportunities to build trust. That's where MAGIC can begin.

CHAPTER 9

Engagement MAGIC®

> The state of mind which enables a man to do work of this kind . . . is akin to that of the religious worshipper or the lover; the daily effort comes from no deliberate intention or program, but straight from the heart."[1]
>
> —Albert Einstein

We accept Employee Engagement as an absolute good, and based on reams of reliable data from our work and that of others, it is. Study after study shows that organizations with engaged employees are more profitable, grow faster, have lower costs, and enjoy lower turnover.

Engagement doesn't end in the workplace. An engaged employee who is having a marvelous EX sees the impact in other areas of her life as well. Her EX continues beyond the walls of her place of employment. At home, she's feeling great about the work she does and its impact on the community. When she's online, she's telling her Facebook friends about the cool things her company is helping her do. When she's on vacation with work 5,000 miles away, she's grateful that her employer respects her leisure time and doesn't ask her to stay connected via phone or email. And if she can't fully cut the phone cord, she checks in willingly.

Some people claim to be able to clearly separate home life and work life. We've found, however, that it doesn't happen for most of us. In fact, that's multiple personality disorder! All sides of our lives are interconnected. What we do at work impacts what happens at home, and vice versa. With work and life so intertwined today, the goal of any enlightened leader should be an EX that turns employees into priceless brand ambassadors wherever they go and whatever they're doing.

That kind of engagement occurs as a result of MAGIC: **M**eaning, **A**utonomy, **G**rowth, **I**mpact, and **C**onnection—the elements essential to a deeply engaged workforce. But what is it? Where does it fit into the engagement-EX picture?

A transformative EX and MAGIC are inseparable. A solid EX is the condition; MAGIC is the collective psychological state that makes that condition possible. When people are fully engaged, they have an extraordinary EX and they experience MAGIC. It's as inevitable as the law of gravity.

> A transformational EX impacts every component of our lives, including life away from work.

So, let's take a closer look at how to create MAGIC.

MAGIC AT THE CENTER

When employees feel that their employer is meeting the promises of the Brand Contract, they *commit* to the organization. When they feel that their employer is meeting the promises of the Transactional Contract, they are satisfied that their basic needs are taken care of and *satisfied* with the organization. When they feel that their employer is meeting the promises of the Psychological Contract, they believe that they are understood, respected, heard, and cared about. They *engage*.

Commitment, Satisfaction, and Engagement are each vital to a healthy organization. You need all three to attain MAGIC and a world-changing EX. Figure 9.1 shows what that EX looks like.

The intersection of Commitment, Satisfaction, and Engagement is the place where all three Contracts are being honored, expectations are clear and aligned, and moments of truth are being managed in a way that creates trust. When all those conditions are met, MAGIC isn't just possible; it's unavoidable.

The trick is, you need all three. Engagement doesn't presuppose MAGIC; we've seen organizations where employees are engaged without having all of the five MAGIC elements present. However, although engaged employees are far less likely to leave an organization than those who are less engaged, even the most engaged team members may look elsewhere for the missing MAGIC keys. An organization where employees are engaged and committed without feeling satisfied will be unstable, because those hygiene factors, like pay, benefits, and advancement, haven't been addressed. In the Age of the Employee, good employees can usually have those satisfaction elements addressed just as easily (and

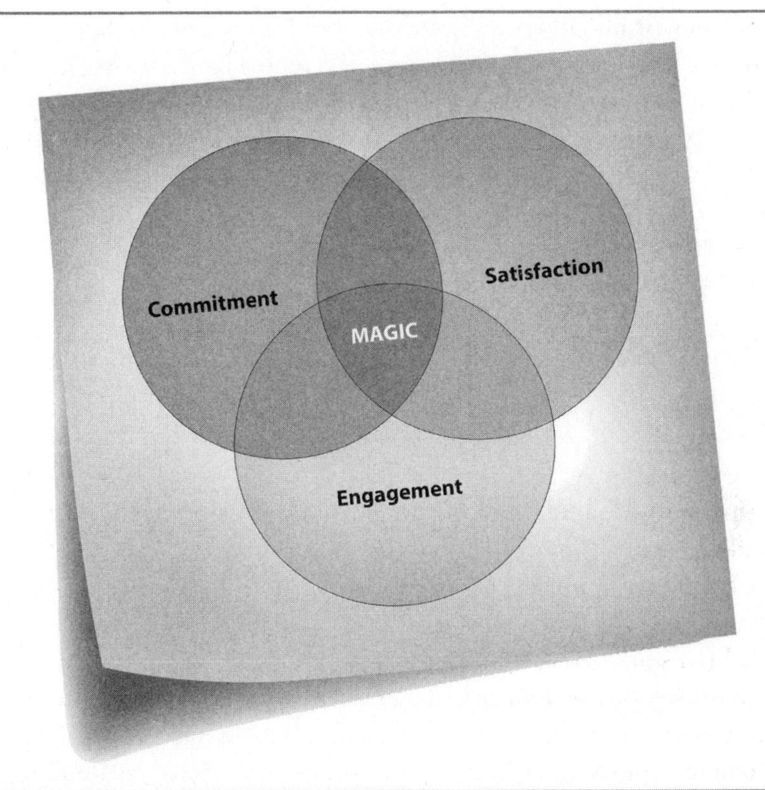

FIGURE 9.1 A MAGIC Intersection: Commitment, Satisfaction, Engagement

possibly better) down the street. With high Satisfaction and Engagement but low Commitment, employees won't really believe in the values and purpose behind the company. And if people are satisfied and committed but not engaged, their passion for the work runs only as deep as the reward for doing it. Take that away, and they stop caring.

CHG, ONE MORE TIME

Fully engaged employees invest their minds, hands, hearts, and spirits in the organization, take ownership of outcomes, and care deeply about delivering the best possible CX. Their "all-in" mentality can transform any company, school, or nonprofit. They drive results.

Earlier in this book, we told you about CHG Healthcare. CHG has MAGIC, and it shows in both their EX and their CX. "Putting People First" isn't just a program or even the company's core corporate value. It's a reflection of the character of the leadership and of the kind of place they want to work, too. EX flows from the values that you and the other leaders hold dear, and those you put into practice. Your people are only as engaged as you are. Engagement is not something you can fake, though plenty of people have tried.

That isn't what a lot of senior executives want to hear. At the elite business schools, they're not talking nearly as much about character, engagement, and vulnerability as they are about marketing, finance, and operations. Few business doctoral candidates are completing their dissertations on "Helping Other People Be Their Best Selves." Yet, the smartest and most successful organizations are building around the expectations and passions of their people, sometimes because they have little choice.

That word—choice—as well as the amount of information available to consumers in every type of enterprise is driving this fundamental shift. Shoppers now have access to huge databases of product reviews and price comparison apps. The health-conscious not only have traditional physician networks and hospitals to choose from, but integrated and natural medicine clinics, health monitoring apps, and online pharmacies. Choice is everywhere, and because it is, everything becomes a commodity. Whatever you're selling or providing in your organization is likely a commodity, too. And in that kind of environment, the one thing that separates you from the competition is your *people.*

Your people deliver the CX. They provide the fantastic service that earns lifetime loyalty. They have brainstorms and create innovations. They're the ones who care enough to step up when things go sideways—for a customer, a patient, a colleague, or even for you.

Your people are your differentiator—in a commoditized world where even category-creating products like the iPhone are copied in a matter of months, they're the only thing that *can* set you apart over the long run. Giving them an optimal, inspiring EX is about maximizing their value, and it doesn't come from salaries and policies. It comes from leaders who care about what the employees care about and help them do what's important to them.

CHG has done that, and we keep coming back to its story because it has done it so well. "We've built a strong foundation: an engaged and trusting environment," says Scott Beck, the CEO. "Over the last year and half, we've been working to develop a higher-level purpose that describes the true value of what we do. This was the result of a collaborative effort and conversations with our employees to better understand where and how they were deriving meaning from their work. It started where we began, with a focus on our people, but it has evolved to include our customers and our communities too. To help bring this new visionary purpose statement to life, we started a recognition program called the Difference Maker Award that celebrates CHG employees that are already making a difference in the world.

"In our first year, we got over sixty nominations and chose four winners. They will take someone important in their lives and join my family and me on our first Difference Makers trip to Kenya. We will be building a school in a village where kids normally wouldn't get to go to school. This is one of the first steps we've taken to express our values outside the company."[2]

That isn't just a strategic initiative designed to generate shiny PR or give employees the warm fuzzies. While it certainly is reflected in the Brand Contract, it also carries over to the Psychological Contract. It's something built into CHG's corporate genetic code because its leaders want to build something that reflects what they care about, too. Their own humanity and that of their employees comes first and makes all their success possible.

"Taking care of people, adding meaning and value beyond the job, making it clear that the company is going to be doing work to give back to the world beyond the commercial value we produce—that's how we've undertaken building a company that's great for our employees *first*," says Scott. "CHG is family. We started by asking 'How do you treat the members of your family or the people who are closest to you?' That's how we treat our employees. They reward us by staying and contributing, and we reward them by helping them achieve what they want to achieve in their lives."[3]

LOOKING THROUGH THE LENS

That "member of your family" perspective that CHG employs is a great example of using the employee lens to understand what matters from people's perspective. We've talked about the lenses—employee, organizational, and leader and the different points of view they provide to leadership. The CHG example shows how valuable that can be. Many organizations persist in a top-down approach not only to management but to culture, which assumes that the same things that are life and death to a Wharton MBA in a corner office are also important to a twenty-five-year-old in the IT department or a single mom with ten years as an administrative assistant.

Sorry. They're not, and building culture from the top-down, organizational lens viewpoint, heedless of what employees are passionate about or what lends meaning to their lives, is a surefire recipe for a disengaged, high-turnover workforce. MAGIC happens when everyone comes together around the same essential values, things like integrity, making a positive difference in the world, environmental responsibility, innovation, or putting family first. No matter what their political or religious backgrounds, 90 percent of the people in any organization will get behind such basic, humanistic values *if* their leaders are genuinely behind them, as well. If these leaders are not, these values are mere window dressing.

According to Kevin Ricklefs, CHG senior vice president of talent management, honoring these values begins with choosing people who fit into the culture you want. "Our first interview is only about cultural fit," he says. "Only the people who pass the cultural test move to skills interviews. We want someone who's a cultural fit with our 'putting people first' belief system. As long as we have that, we can train them on the vast majority of jobs. When you create fit, your people create your culture. When you help to create the culture, you tend to be more connected to it. As the business environment and economy change, we need to change, and our people help us do that."[4]

Of course, that philosophy doesn't just apply to the rank and file. Leaders, all the way to the C-suite, need to fit with the culture, too.

"Our culture is built on teamwork, communication, and openness, and our leaders have to fit into it, too," says Mark Law, CHG's chief operating officer. "We look for leaders who are willing to see their job as helping their people be successful. It's not a power leadership culture. It's a coaching, teaching leadership culture. That's why it's hard to be a leader here. Command and control is easy. It's more challenging to lead when it's about helping and nurturing."[5]

The lenses are invaluable tools for figuring out what your people care about and how you can tap into those values to build a stronger, more engaged culture at all levels, from leaders to new hires. Looking through the employee lens reveals what employees think and believe about what the organization is doing and what it *should* be doing. Those beliefs reveal what's important to employees. Looking through the organizational lens reveals ways that leadership can accommodate employees' values and beliefs in ways that also benefit the organization. Looking through the leader lens shows how to integrate both employee and organizational lenses to create *fit* . . . and MAGIC.

LIFE'S WORC

Without the lenses, the quest for MAGIC can be a guessing game. That's the lesson behind Life's WORC, a nonprofit organization that provides care for people with developmental disabilities in the New York City metro area. Life's WORC was chosen for the 2016 Achievers 50 Most Engaged Workplaces Award, but things haven't always been so good. Launched in 1971 to provide alternatives to traditional institutions for people with developmental disabilities, Life's WORC grew quickly. But by 1995, it had gone through six CEOs in ten years, the result of a toxic internal environment where no one trusted anybody.

Leadership began casting about for solutions that would improve culture and reduce the 40 percent turnover rate. A Total Quality Management approach improved processes and efficiency but didn't affect the culture or how employees saw Life's WORC. Finally, in 1999, the leaders decided to focus on values. They created a Values Committee and asked the nonprofit's 500 employees, "What do we believe in? What are the values that, if lived, would make this a great place to work at and result in high-quality services?" The goal was to build a team, reduce conflict, and create a sense of trust.

By now, knowing how we think, you're probably reading this with the same skepticism we had, because you know it's not that easy. And it wasn't. But Life's WORC management team kept plugging along. They collected data and spent 18 months analyzing it to determine the organization's core values, based—and this is the key—on what *employees* valued. Management saw through the employee lens and let that insight drive leadership behavior.

Once they understood the core values, the management team worked to change the culture, starting with senior leaders. As one said: "I saw a real change. Initially I was a tyrant and then amazingly over five or six years it changed . . . I had to fight to not be the way I was to become something a little softer and nicer, and that worked."[6]

Eventually, through annual surveys and ongoing employee discussions, Life's WORC collected huge amounts of data and used it to transform everything about the organization's culture and brand, from increasing training and coaching to proactively addressing the dangers of workplace gossip. Employee engagement survey scores soared. Turnover dropped to 15 percent. Employees at every level enjoyed greater autonomy and educational opportunities.

Today, Life's WORC is one of the most engaged organizations in North America. It's an inspiring story that shows that by approaching problems from the right perspective (which isn't always management's perspective) and being persistent, it's possible to transform even the most dysfunctional organization.

To put it simply, human nature isn't to wake up in the morning saying, "I sure hope today stinks." We *want* and *need* to engage. MAGIC wants to happen.

MAGIC wants to happen.

EX AND THE FIVE ELEMENTS

In our previous book, *MAGIC: Five Keys to Unlock the Power of Employee Engagement*, we revealed the results of our research involving over 14 million employee survey responses. Since that time, we've added more than 10 million additional responses, giving us a pretty clear idea of what creates a brilliant EX. These results supported what we suspected: MAGIC and EX are inseparable. They go hand-in-hand.

A stellar EX is both a cause of *and* a result of MAGIC: Meaning, Autonomy, Growth, Impact, and Connection. When these five keys are present, your people will engage in ways you can't even imagine. So, let's look at the various pieces of EX to see how they relate directly to MAGIC.

Meaning

Meaning occurs when employees believe that their work serves an important purpose beyond that of a company's profitability or other metrics. The key is that each employee must find that purpose important *at a personal level.* Meaning is different for each individual.

The Brand Contract comes into play because it broadcasts the organization's culture and values. Consider Patagonia, which we looked at earlier. The company's brand pivots on an ironclad commitment to ecological stewardship that attracts employees who fit the culture; that commitment lends meaning to their work.

The Psychological Contract implies what the organization believes and cares about. It's a promise to employees that working for the organization will fulfill their emotional and other needs, not just give them an income. This is where the character of the leaders has to be consistent with what they are saying and doing. People find meaning in work that serves what they care about.

Kairos moments are the third key ingredient in Meaning because they tend to reflect the character and values embodied in the Psychological Contract. Because unpredictable events reveal who people really are, they will reveal the authenticity (or lack thereof) of leaders' commitment to things like integrity, putting employees first, and giving back. Leaders who want their people to have Meaning will ensure that the values they espouse publicly are also those they can live with privately, especially when caught off guard by a crisis or a conflict.

Autonomy

Autonomy is the power to shape your work and environment in ways that allow you to perform at your best. This doesn't mean, however, that employees are left to complete control and anarchy. The Transactional Contract is important because it provides the necessary boundaries for Autonomy to exist. Whether it's express or implied, you're telling employees that they will be given opportunities to be self-starters—to use their talents, abilities, and good judgment to drive results. That creates expectations that then must be met on both sides.

It's not hard to see how Expectation Alignment (EA) is a precursor to Autonomy. If you let people know that they will be counted on to be self-directed and independent, they are far more likely to strive to exhibit those qualities and to take pride in meeting those expectations. When you give them autonomy as promised, they will feel respected and engaged. Also, as we saw with ALDI, having the Transactional Contract firmly in place defines the boundaries of the playing field. A culture of Autonomy says "here are the rules and field of play, now take the ball and run with it."

Finally, the Brand Contract plays a role here because independence and the freedom to work in a way that suits employees—whether that means telecommuting or something as radical as the Zappos holacracy experiment—is a huge part of any organization's brand promise, especially to incoming employees. If your culture promises Autonomy, even in subtle ways, you'd better be prepared to encourage and support it. If your culture promises strong supervision, guidance, mentoring, and hand-holding, deliver that or face the consequences.

Growth

Growth is simple to define. It's being stretched and challenged in ways that result in personal and professional progress. Our research into engagement has shown us that the desire for growth has more impact on EX today than it ever has in the past. Employees, particularly younger employees, are joining (and leaving) organizations because of Growth possibilities (think Google, where thousands of prospective employees are looking for opportunities to learn, not to mention a bullet on a résumé). That's a powerful Brand Contract.

As with Autonomy, the Transactional Contract and Expectation Alignment are both important for Growth because they speak to the evolution of employees' roles and their ambitions. We want our people to stretch and aspire to bigger things but to do it in ways that don't stretch them too far or too fast, beyond the breaking point. That's where the Transactional Contract can clearly spell out the opportunities for growth and when and under what conditions employees can expect to find them. This is an area where written and verbal Contracts can work in tandem.

The written Contract may state that the employee will have a performance review in one year, at which time a promotion is possible. Then, after onboarding, the boss talks about opportunities for training and development available to ambitious employees who turn in a great proposal, come up with a cost-saving idea, or demonstrate abilities and desires.

The Contract also creates expectations, and now the leadership team needs to make sure expectations are aligned by helping employees find the growth opportunities that were promised. Managers aren't responsible for seeing that employees take *advantage* of the opportunities, just that those opportunities are available.

This is also a good time to take a look through the employee lens to find out what type of growth your employees find most meaningful. Some managers may be surprised that, for many employees, Growth doesn't always equal a promotion and bump in salary. For many, it could be learning new skills or becoming an elite-level talent at skills they already possess.

Chronos moments come into play with Growth in a big way because of milestones like performance reviews, work anniversaries, and other markers that cause employees to stop, reflect, and assess where they are in their careers. Employers should be peering through the employee lens regularly to see when those moments are coming and to ensure that when they arrive, employees feel like they have at least been given opportunities for growth.

Impact

Contracts take center stage with Impact because in order to do impactful work, employees often need the cooperation of their employer. Impact involves seeing positive, effective, and worthwhile outcomes and results from one's work.

The Brand Contract sets the ground state expectation that the organization cares about work that makes customers' lives better, helps patients be healthier, or what have you. Further, the organization lets employees know that this is an organization where the employee can make a difference—whatever that difference may be.

Mission statements, charitable giving, community outreach programs, customer feedback channels—all this and more can be used to bolster the organization's brand as aspiring to make an impact on the world. However, the biggest impact comes from action. Shaping employee perceptions is fine, as long as there's honest, sincere effort on the part of leadership to really have an impact—and not just on the bottom line.

A strong Psychological Contract supports employees' belief that leaders are sincere and honest in their intentions to have a positive impact on the world, the community, or individual lives. Since this Contract has more to do with who a person promises to be than what someone promises to do, its effect on Impact has everything to do with how leaders honor the spirit of employees' desire for their work to make a difference. Do they provide ways to build relationships with customers? Do they listen to concerns about issues that, at first glance, have nothing to do with the bottom line? Are they receptive to changes in the organizational model that might temporarily affect sales or productivity but make the organization a better citizen of the world? Do they back up their words with action or just say "We care" and do nothing?

When we conduct Employee Engagement surveys, we typically ask employees to rate their agreement with the statement "I can see how the work I do has an impact on the success of the organization." Interestingly, nearly one-third of employees don't make the connection between what they do and how it helps the organization succeed. Think of the power that could be harnessed if all employees were able to connect the dots between their roles, their EXs, and the organization's results, whether that means life-saving products, award-winning CX, or feeding a child in a remote village.

Connection

Connection is a sense of belonging to something greater than oneself. Rather than an EX that says "put in your eight hours and go home," a sense of Connection says, "come be a part of something great."

As it does in every other area, the Brand Contract communicates the core values and culture of the organization. Culture is essential, but not for the reasons you might think. Having an open, warm, and friendly culture is wonderful, but it's more important that your Brand Contract portray your culture accurately. If you're an engineer-driven company that's serious about technology, and not into goofy parties, fine. Be open about that. There are people who will connect within almost any kind of organizational culture, as long as that culture is portrayed honestly and employees are treated fairly.

Because it deals in beliefs, emotions, and relationships, the Psychological Contract has more power here than in any other element of MAGIC. Your employees should not just feel like a band of brothers with each other; they should feel the same about their leaders and the organization as well. In the best organizations, entry-level employees feel some kinship with the upper levels of the organization—they feel heard, respected, understood, and valued. That's the state your Psychological Contract should be fostering.

If you have all that in place, Kairos moments should be a walk in the park. If people feel like they are part of a family where everyone has a voice and where the leaders really care about helping people reach their full potential, those unpredictable moments of truth will pretty much take care of themselves.

THE EX AND MAGIC

MAGIC creates an exceptional Employee Experience. An exceptional EX glows with MAGIC. As long as their basic needs for pay, recognition, tools and resources, safety, and other hygiene factors are taken care of, MAGIC can grow, and employees will need little else to provide a spectacular experience for customers. That will transform any organization.

However, that can happen only in organizations that treat the EX as a human phenomenon, something built on feelings, confidence, and the desire to excel. It isn't transactional, and it isn't about satisfaction issues like vacation time or medical leave. Those are important, and they need to be present for a great EX, but they won't produce that EX on their own.

So to close out this chapter, let's look at what the EX is *not*:

- It's not the Employee Life Cycle (ELC), which accounts for the steps or processes in which an employee participates during his or her relationship with an organization. The ELC is chronological and sequential, with a beginning and an end. It takes into account important events and processes, such as recruiting, onboarding, employee development, promotion, exit interviews, and so on, and it starts with an employee's first contact with an organization to his or her last interaction after termination. EX is the responsibility of each leader and employee, while much of the responsibility for the ELC is the purview of HR.
- It's not a set of perks, like foosball tables and free beverages in the break room. Perks are easy (although often costly) to implement, and make employees feel good during the short-term, but they don't solve core business problems or address emotional needs or expectations.

- It's not the Employee Value Proposition (EVP). EVP, which is a part of the EX, examines all the areas of value that impact an employee's decision to join, stay, become and remain engaged, and drive results. These could be everything from paying for continuing education to parental leave to radical brand-reinforcing moves like REI's Black Friday closure. While EVP is an important part of the EX, it does not encompass the EX.
- It's not talent management or HR development. These are about everything from fit to training, and represent, in a way, what the organization does *to* employees. While talent management and HR initiatives are certainly important, they are only part of the larger EX.

So what is the EX in our world? It's the totality of what employees encounter and believe about their interactions with their organization and its leaders.

As we said, beliefs shape everything: emotions, thoughts, and behavior. Trust is a belief that you're as good as your word and that your intentions are honorable. Commitment is a belief that your organization is worth the employee's time—that you are trying to live up to each employee's ideal. Connection is a belief that it's safe to give your all to an organization because the people at all levels root for and understand each other. Even EA is a belief—a belief that the organization is constant in what it says and does, that it does not change with every gust.

The EX isn't just the good times when everyone feels purposeful and business is easy. It's also the days where there are difficult performance reviews, or when things just aren't going well. It takes shape based on how a manager supports an employee the day she learns her mother has cancer. It pivots on how well leaders address employee concerns following the last employee engagement survey, or how they deal with conflict.

The EX is everything that influences the meaning of work, people's feelings of autonomy and empowerment, a culture that encourages growth in personally important ways, opportunities to make and see a positive impact on the world, and the ability to connect with people at all levels in ways that enhance everyone's lives. If you have all of that, you have MAGIC. Let's close by looking at how we make an extraordinary, this-changes-everything EX happen.

CHAPTER 9. ENGAGEMENT MAGIC: THE CHAPTER EXPERIENCE

- Employee Engagement goes hand in hand with an Employee Experience that makes customers love your organization.
- MAGIC—Meaning, Autonomy, Growth, Impact, and Connection—is the collection of five keys that make engagement not only possible, but optimal.
- You can have engagement without MAGIC, but it's weaker, more fragile, and generally not sustainable. With MAGIC, engagement leads to a stellar EX.
- MAGIC lives at the intersection of Satisfaction, Commitment, and Engagement. You must have all three to have MAGIC.
- MAGIC depends largely on the personal qualities and actions of leaders—their character, values, and integrity.
- The components of the EX—Expectation Alignment, the three Contracts, and the Chronos and Kairos moments of truth—matter to different parts of MAGIC in different ways.
- The Employee Experience is the sum of perceptions employees have about their interactions with the organization in which they work. In the end, the EX is everything your employees believe about your organization.

CHAPTER 10

Building the EXtraordinary

> Make no little plans; they have no magic to stir men's blood. . . . Make big plans: aim high in hope and work.
>
> —DANIEL BURNHAM, U.S. ARCHITECT (1846–1912)

Once upon a time there was a big company. It was a major player in the technology world and, by every measure, it was a success. But company leaders were concerned. To them, the company culture felt stodgy and stale. Leaders of the organization wanted to refresh it, to make the company a place where people wanted to work. So it created the People Deal, the embodiment of the experience it wanted people to have.

The Deal outlined what employees could expect from the company and what the company expected of employees. At the heart of the People Deal was the theme of "connection." For its people, that meant employees could expect to be connected to people, information, and opportunities they needed for success. In return, the company expected employees to align their work with both business goals and customer needs.

That company? Cisco Systems, the behemoth at the heart of much of the tech world's infrastructure. If the world's largest networking company, with more than 70,000 employees, felt that culture is vital enough to engage in a major engagement program, it's probably a big deal. And Cisco did it right: with creativity, alignment of expectations, respect for its people, and total commitment.

ASKING THE RIGHT QUESTIONS

If you've come this far, you're ready to use the tools we have given you to cultivate and grow an extraordinary Employee Experience. But what does an extraordinary EX look like? It's different for every organization, of course, but there are some common threads, whether you are running a for-profit corporation, a religious organization or a hospital, or small team of five people.

When employees are having an extraordinary experience, they integrate their work and their lives effortlessly. Work is meaningful and enjoyable instead of draining and punishing, so there's no need for ongoing discussions about improving work-life balance. Work is something to savor, not recover from. They take ownership not only of outcomes but of your culture, because it's something they actively create in real time by virtue of their ideas and actions. They care deeply about each other, leading to that band-of-brothers, walk-through-fire atmosphere that's so powerful and desirable.

Just as important, they deliver an incredible Customer Experience (CX), which is where the rubber really meets the road. The point of any organization, after all, is to achieve its goals: profitability if it's a corporation, student success and a sustainable endowment if it's a university. Thrilling customers (or students, patients, or donors, as the case may be) and earning their love and allegiance is the key to those goals, and employees are the custodians of the CX.

You know if your people are crushing the CX because you'll hear about it. Your customers will let you know when they're being taken care of, when they feel heard and responded to, and when people are going above and beyond the call. Remember the Law of Congruent Experience, EX = CX? It's at work here. Give your people an exceptional work experience, and they will do the same for the people you serve. You'll see that manifest in more repeat business, higher satisfaction scores, more referrals and recommendations, and a healthier bottom line.

The real work of crafting and growing that kind of EX begins, as most worthwhile things do, with asking the right questions. As you have noticed in our examinations of engaged organizations where there is clearly an outstanding EX, the leaders are men and women who care deeply about people and are humble enough to ask questions and go where the answers lead.

If you're looking for a way to start creating the kind of EX you can boast about, start there. Some questions we recommend:

- What kinds of expectations are we creating in our people?
- Are they realistic? Are they clear? If not, why not?

- How are we living up to these expectations, and where are we failing to do so?
- How is our alignment, and are we considering the Six EA Pillars? What do our Brand, Transactional, and Psychological Contracts promise?
- Is everyone aware of the terms of those Contracts?
- Did we inherit a Contract from previous leadership?
- How can we amend our Contract, and should we?
- Which lenses are we looking through?
- How have we handled our moments of truth, and how will we handle them in the future?

> Give your people an exceptional work experience and you'll see the fruits manifest in more repeat business, higher satisfaction scores, more referrals and recommendations, and a healthier bottom line.

BREAD CRUMBS

When you have begun answering those questions (or questions that you devise on your own), it's also time to start walking through the process we've outlined in this book—the process of laying the groundwork for your own organization-shaping EX. Make no mistake, it *is* a process; you can follow a predictable, linear path all the way from the Expectation Gap to MAGIC and beyond, to the customer. It's like having Hansel and Gretel's bread crumbs to guide you home so you never lose your way. The elements look like this:

Expectation Alignment * Three Contracts *

Moments of Truth * MAGIC * EX

It might seem complicated, but think of each stage as a stepping-stone on the way to an exceptional EX. Just follow the stones and you'll reach your goal without getting wet.

OLIVIA'S EX

Remember Olivia, our fictional employee from earlier in the book? Let's use her experience to track the progress of the EX from the beginning of our linear process to the end. If you remember, she was hired and promised an office and advancement, and then was disappointed when neither materialized. When we last saw our heroine, she was asking friends about other jobs and her employer was at risk of losing her.

But before it's too late, her boss, Paolo, steps up and talks with her candidly. Olivia expresses her frustration and disillusionment with how she's been treated. Paolo tells her that the following week, she will be moved into an office, given a raise in keeping with her excellent performance, and sent to training to learn some important financial skills. Paolo apologizes for the misstep, letting her know that this move was overdue. What's more, in her new position she may have the opportunity to lead several important project teams later in the year.

Olivia is delighted and decides to stay. Critically, she has a set of new expectations for her time at the company. Paolo makes clear his expectations for her: work hard in her training sessions, continue to take on new responsibilities, and lead others by displaying the company's key values of integrity, assertiveness, and customer empathy.

EXPECTATION ALIGNMENT

What Olivia doesn't know is that Paolo, as well as others on the team, consider her to be management material, and not only want to keep her at the company but groom her for something more. Conscious of the promises he has made and the expectations Olivia has formed, he does his level best to deliver what he pledged. Olivia moves into an office, gets a pay increase and a new title, and is given more responsibility.

Critically, however, the chance to lead project teams does not materialize as promised. Frustrated, Olivia asks her boss about this. He says that things simply have been too busy to initiate the project that he had in mind for her to direct. However, there are several new hires coming into her department in the coming month; would she like to supervise their orientation and in-house training? That would give her some leadership and management experience.

Olivia gladly consents to train the rookies. Some of her expectations have been met, while others have not. However, her most important expectation—that the company will deal with her honestly, transparently, and with good intentions—has been reinforced.

Expectation Alignment: Not perfect, but good.

THREE CONTRACTS

Olivia begins training the new recruits. As she does, she notices that although two women who have just been hired have even stronger résumés than the two men, they are being paid less for very similar jobs. This perplexes her; when she was researching the company before interviewing, one of the things she liked about it was its talk about opportunity and equal pay for women. That was a strong part of its Brand Contract, but now she wonders if that Contract was a marketing ploy to get people in the door.

Despite this, her trainees thrive, and when their orientation period is over, they write glowing reviews of her work as a mentor. Olivia doesn't see the reviews, of course, but Paolo congratulates her on a job well done, and gives her the reinforcing feedback. She looks forward eagerly to her next performance review and to finally getting a chance to lead a project team, something that was promised nearly a year before.

However, as the time for her review approaches, silence. The company is expanding and Paolo is traveling constantly.

Then she gets an email from him: He's stuck in meetings in Tokyo, but can they do her performance review by videoconference? She looks at the time of the proposed meeting and realizes that with the time difference, her boss will have to be awake at 3 a.m. She declines, and says she can wait for him to get home. But the gesture alone, and the fact that Paolo was willing to inconvenience himself so much to do her review, makes her feel that her Transactional Contract has been satisfied somewhat.

Later, Paolo returns from Asia and they do her review face to face. It's stellar. Olivia not only gets her project team, but her boss tells her how much the whole company appreciates her patience and hard work during a busy time. She walks out of his office a mile off the ground, believing that the company really does value her—as well as the other women in the firm.

Brand Contract: Shaky, but okay.
Transactional Contract: Strong.
Psychological Contract: Off the charts.

MOMENTS OF TRUTH

A year goes by and Olivia not only leads a project team, she excels. She's promoted to a departmental management position and put in charge of a team of six. Because she is such a rising star, her new boss, Angelica, has told her that she will be asked to speak at the company's next worldwide retreat in New York. She's thrilled and starts preparing for her speech three months in advance. But then she begins to worry.

Unfortunately, the company has gone back on big promises in the past—not out of ill intentions, but because it just can't seem to get itself organized. This time, however, her fears are groundless. At the conference, she goes to the podium and gets a standing ovation. This moment of truth (MOT) goes off without a hitch.

Back home, she takes charge of a larger team, including three women. But when it's time for annual compensation reviews, she finds more worrisome pay disparities between the women and the men. Frustrated by this, she brings her concerns to the vice president of HR. He thanks her for bringing it to his attention, tells her not to worry about it, then nothing happens for the rest of the year. Olivia's trust in the organization is damaged, perhaps irreparably.

Chronos Moment of Truth: Perfect.
Kairos Moment of Truth: Disaster.

MAGIC

At this point, we can assess Olivia's Employee Experience by looking at how she feels in each of the five components of MAGIC. Remember, MAGIC has direct ties to EX.

Olivia has enjoyed strong Expectation Alignment and felt that her Contracts were mostly upheld. But her Moment of Truth around women's pay was devastating. Did MAGIC survive? Let's see.

Meaning. Olivia cares about her work, but in the last year, part of the meaning behind the work came from ensuring that all employees were given fair opportunities in the company. That cause appears lost now.

Autonomy. She has autonomy, but still feels undervalued because her concerns were brushed aside. She feels powerless to make things right.

Growth. Olivia has grown, and she is grateful. New opportunities continue to come her way regularly, and she has taken advantage of them.

Impact. Olivia enjoys the impact she is having on customers more than any other part of the job. She is making a difference.

Connection. This is the big casualty. Any connection Olivia felt to the company was gone the moment her concerns about equal pay were dismissed. She feels betrayed.

MAGIC: Sadly, it may be hanging by a thread.
Olivia has started to disengage from her job.

THE CUSTOMER EXPERIENCE

With MAGIC weak, what was once a positive, inspiring EX has become marked by regret, resentment, and possibly even the desire to work elsewhere. Because Olivia is dedicated, she tries to soldier on and give her customers the best possible experience, but they can tell her heart isn't in it, as can her team. Eventually, she tells one that she's looking for another position, and he immediately offers her a job. She accepts and, four weeks later, she's gone.

Management is tempted to diminish the impact by quoting the mantra "We've lost them before and we'll lose them again." Yet, in today's economy, great talent might be the difference between success or obscurity.

But, we're all about happy endings, right? So let's look at an alternative ending to our story. Just as our heroine is about to push "send" on her email to the recruiter that has been pestering her, she gets a call from the CEO, who invites her to participate in his new pet project, "It takes a village." As one of the components of this project, he has asked Olivia to take the lead on solving the pay equity issues around the company.

That changes things. Connection may still be tenuous, and Olivia is taking a wait-and-see approach, but there's certainly room for hope.

The lesson of our little fable (both endings)? EX and engagement vary over time. Trust is fragile. Leaders need to renew it again and again by meeting expectations, understanding and managing their Contracts, and being consistent with their values when moments of truth arise.

To put it another way, the price of Employee Engagement is eternal vigilance. A great EX requires a Zen-like commitment on the part of leaders.

THREE INGREDIENTS

We have shared the stories of a number of organizations with you in the course of this book. They're all very different, with diverse histories, leaders, and visions of what success means. But they—and all organizations with extraordinary Employee Experiences—have in common a few qualities that we'd like to share with you before we part ways.

The first is *mindfulness.* Great EX architects are hyperaware of how what they do impacts what employees expect, believe, and feel about their work and the people they work with. Going through your career cosseted in a corner office, distant from the concerns of the people who make things run, is a sure way to fail. How do your actions shape culture and values? How do others perceive you? Has your leadership fallen into patterns that work against engagement and an exceptional EX? Being mindful doesn't mean being critical, but it does mean being willing to question your unconscious behavior and the effect it may be having on your people.

The second is *curiosity.* Leaders who build a world-class EX do so in part because they're unquenchably curious about what makes their employees tick and what makes them happy. They care about the people they work with, no matter what level they're at or how long they've been on the team. They're fascinated by what compels people to give their all to a cause, and they recognize that it's not money or title. They're always asking, investigating, tweaking, and testing to discover the key to helping people feel great about what they do and take ownership of projects, customers, and the organization. They are never, ever satisfied, and in a good way. Sound like fun?

Finally, EX geniuses are *persistent.* As we saw with Life's WORC, changing culture and growing engagement isn't always fast and easy. In fact, if it's going to be organic, it can't be. Ultimately, employees create culture and choose to engage; managers create the optimal conditions for that to happen.

Results can be slow and frustrating. Programs can flop or yield results that are less than thrilling. But you keep plugging away, trying new things and learning what you can from every initiative. Eventually, as we've seen, if you're listening and empathetic, and open to having your preconceptions turned upside down, you will get results.

Successful organizations attract talent, retain top performers, and create environments where people are engaged to drive results. It comes down to the Employee Experience. If you care about your people and helping them be the best they can be, they will do the same for your organization. And what will that do for your own, very personal EX?

So get to it.

APPENDIX

Comparing the Three Contracts: Brand, Transactional, and Psychological

Brand Contract	Transactional Contract	Psychological Contract
• Both intentionally and unintentionally generated; while we may want to be in control of this, we often are not • Image-focused; based primarily on perception • Can be greatly influenced by others who are not part of the relationship • Fluid and changing, can swing based on the involvement and input of others • Relies heavily on the past; little intentional anticipatory effect (not intended to anticipate future potential actions) • Is often developed before the formal relationship begins • Is the reason why we are attracted by and to the relationship • Adjusted based on ongoing experiences; all parties expect this contract to be renegotiated over time	• Focused on short-term exchanges and specific cases; quid-pro-quo • Explicit (but not always written); agreed upon by all parties with an attempt to minimize misinterpretation • Promissory: Based on an exchange of reciprocal bilateral commitments • Compliance-focused; breaches are closely monitored by both sides • The default setting: If there is ever a problem, we revert back to the transactional contact • Intended to bind parties together through preserving mutual interests • Inclusive: Considers both parties' wants and needs • Intentional, tangible, and quantifiable • Emphasizes fairness of the procedural outcome and equality • Breaches are mutually understood and identifiable; renegotiated through agreement on both sides • Forward-looking and anticipatory	• Implicit; terms and desires of the contract may be discussed explicitly, but the honoring of that contract is left to interpretation • Non-reciprocal: Generally does not involve a "this-for-that" exchange • Both parties pay attention to the fairness of the process, rather than to the fairness of the outcomes • Open-ended • Based on beliefs and perceptions of obligations on each side • Unilateral; not mutually agreed-upon • Dynamic: Constantly being rewritten, often based on changes in the state of one or both parties • Can withstand short-term violations if the long-term investment is perceived to be worthwhile • Violation of the contract is largely perceptual and often unnoticed by the other party • Holistic: Viewed by parties as a whole, rather than as individual components

Notes

INTRODUCTION

1. J. Meister, "Airbnb Chief Human Resource Officer Becomes Chief Employee Experience Officer," *Forbes*, July 21, 2015. Retrieved from http://www.forbes.com/sites/jeannemeister/2015/07/21/airbnbs-chief-human-resource-officer-becomes-chief-employee-experience-officer/
2. J. Morgan , "Why the Future of Work Is All About the Employee Experience," *Forbes*, May 27, 2015. Retrieved from http://www.forbes.com/sites/jacobmorgan/2015/05/27/why-the-future-of-work-is-all-about-the-employee-experience/

CHAPTER 1

1. M. Schmidt-Subramanian and G. Fleming, "The Revenue Impact of Customer Experience," August 11, 2015. Retrieved from https://www.forrester.com/report/The+Revenue+Impact+Of+Customer+Experience+2015/-/E-RES122323
2. James L. Heskett, Thomas O. Jones, Gary W. Loveman, W. Earl Sasser, Jr., and Leonard A. Schlesinger, "Putting the Service-Profit Chain to Work," *Harvard Business Review* (July-August 2008).
3. RnR Market Research, "Customer Experience Management Market by Touch Points (Company Website, Ranch/Store, Web, and Call Center), by Regions (North America, Europe, Asia-Pacific, Middle East & Africa, and Latin America), by Vertical (IT Communication Service Providers, BFSI, and Others)—Global Forecast to 2020." Retrieved from http://www.marketsandmarkets.com/PressReleases/customer-experience-management.asp
4. American Customer Satisfaction Index, "Customer Satisfaction Benchmarks." Retrieved from http://www.theacsi.org/
5. Stefan Tornquist, "The Consumer Conversation," *Econsultancy* (April 2014). Retrieved from https://econsultancy.com/reports/the-consumer-conversation/
6. Accenture, "B2B Customer Experience: Start Playing to Win and Stop Playing Not to Lose," June 12, 2014. Retrieved from https://www.accenture.com/us-en/~/media/Accenture/Conversion-Assets/DotCom/Documents/Global/PDF/Strategy_6/Accenture-B2B-Customer-Experience-Start-Playing-Win-Stop-Playing-Not-Lose.pdf
7. Jaime Estupinan, Ashish Kaura, and Keith Fengler, "The Birth of the Healthcare Consumer: Growing Demands for . . ." *Strategy&*, October 14, 2014.

8. Jon Hilkevitch, "Ventra Boss 'Can't Guess' When New Fare System Will Work," *Chicago Tribune*, November 6, 2013. Retrieved from http://articles.chicagotribune.com/2013-11-06/news/chi-cta-chief-ventra-developer-must-correct-poor-customer-experiences-20131105_1_ventra-accounts-ventra-contract-cta-president-forrest-claypool
9. Rick Perlstein, "Chicago's 'Smart Card' Debacle and Privatisation," *The Nation*, December 10, 2013. Retrieved from https://www.thenation.com/article/chicagos-smart-card-debacle-and-privatisation/
10. Michael Hinshaw, "Customer Experience Lessons from the Chicago Transit Authority: A Cautionary Tale," *CMO*, November 19, 2013. Retrieved from http://www.cmo.com/opinion/articles/2013/11/19/customer_experience_.html
11. Chuck Sudo, "A Former Ventra Call Center Employee Speaks," *Chicagoist*, December 17, 2013. Retrieved from http://chicagoist.com/2013/12/17/a_former_ventra_call_center_employe.php
12. "Three Is Our Magic Number," *YouTube*, March 14, 2014. https://www.youtube.com/watch?v=2lOLXPFsZ58
13. Susan Sorenson, "Lower Your Health Costs While Boosting Performance," *Business Journal*, September 19, 2013. Retrieved from http://www.gallup.com/businessjournal/164420/lower-health-costs-boosting-performance.aspx
14. "Over 50% of US Workers Are Thinking About a New Job for the New Year," *Indeed Blog*, January 14, 2016. Retrieved from http://blog.indeed.com/2016/01/14/new-job-for-the-new-year/
15. Oscar Raymundo, "Richard Branson: Companies Should Put Employees First," *Inc.*, October 28, 2014. Retrieved from http://www.inc.com/oscar-raymundo/richard-branson-companies-should-put-employees-first.html
16. James B. Stewart, "Ousted Founder of Men's Wearhouse Watches His Old Company Struggle," *New York Times*, November 25, 2015. Retrieved from http://www.nytimes.com/2015/11/27/business/george-zimmer-former-face-of-mens-wearhouse-watches-his-old-company-struggle.html?_r=0

CHAPTER 2

1. *Frigaliment Importing Co. v. B.N.S. International Sales Corp.* case brief summary; 190 F. Supp. 116 (1960). Retrieved from www.lawschoolcasebriefs.net/search?q=frigaliment
2. *Hawkins v. McGee;* Hairy Hand case; (Sup. Ct. of NH, 1929); Supp 10; Notes 2. Retrieved from www.lawschoolcasebriefs.net/2012/03/hawkins-v-mcgee-case-brief.html
3. NPR Staff, "The Superintendent Who Turned Around a School District," January 3, 2016. Retrieved from www.npr.org/2016/01/03/461205086/the-superintendent-who-turned-around-a-school-district

4. Tiffany Anderson, "Breaking the Cycle of Poverty," *District Administration Magazine*, December 2015. Used with permission. Retrieved from www.districtadministration.com/article/1215-Anderson
5. R. C. Huseman, J. D. Hatfield, and E. W. Miles, "A New Perspective on Equity Theory: The Equity Sensitivity Construct," *Academy of Management Review* 12, no. 2 (1987): 222–234. doi:10.5465/amr.1987.4307799
6. James K. McNulty, "Positive Expectations in the Early Years of Marriage: Should Couples Expect the Best or Brace for the Worst?" *Journal of Personality and Social Psychology* 86, no. 5 (2004): 729–743.

CHAPTER 3

1. J. Kantor and D. Streitfeld, "Inside Amazon: Wrestling Big Ideas in a Bruising Workplace," *New York Times*, August 15, 2015. Retrieved from http://www.nytimes.com/2015/08/16/technology/inside-amazon-wrestling-big-ideas-in-a-bruising-workplace.html
2. M. Saito, "Amazon Chief Bezos Defends Corporate Culture in Letter to Shareholders," April 6, 2016. Retrieved from http://www.reuters.com/article/us-amazon-com-bezos-idUSKCN0X302C
3. J. Bezos, "Amazon Letter to Shareholders," 1997. Retrieved from https://www.sec.gov/Archives/edgar/data/1018724/000119312516530910/d168744dex991.htm
4. Cat Zakrzewski, "Amazon's Work/Life Balance Lags Other Tech Companies, Study Says," *Wall Street Journal*, August 25, 2015.
5. "DecisionWise 2016 Leadership Intelligence 360-degree Feedback Benchmark Analysis Report," DecisionWise, LLC.
6. J. Henley, "Long Lunch: Spanish Civil Servant Skips Work for Years without Anyone Noticing," *The Guardian*, February 12, 2016. Retrieved from https://www.theguardian.com/world/2016/feb/12/long-lunch-spanish-civil-servant-skips-work-for-years-without-anyone-noticing
7. "Gen Y and Gen Z Global Workplace Expectations Study," September 2, 2014. Retrieved from http://millennialbranding.com/2014/geny-genz-global-workplace-expectations-study/
8. Jennifer Reingold, "The Zappos Experiment," *Fortune*, March 15, 2016.
9. S. R. Covey, "7 Habits of Highly Effective People: Habit 5: Seek First to Understand, Then to Be Understood." Retrieved from https://www.stephencovey.com/7habits/7habits-habit5.php
10. http://lexicon.ft.com/Term?term=audit-expectation-gap
11. Allison Van Dusen, "The Emotional Impact of the Wall Street Crisis," *Forbes*, September 15, 2008. Retrieved from http://www.forbes.com/2008/09/15/lehman-health-emotion-forbeslife-cx_avd_0915emotionlehman.html

12. William Cohan, "Deaths Draw Attention to Wall Street's Grueling Pace," *New York Times*, October 3, 2015. Retrieved from http://www.nytimes.com/2015/10/04/business/dealbook/tragedies-draw-attention-to-wall-streets-grueling-pace.html
13. Leslie Pickler, "Goldman Sachs Rolls Out New Policies to Retain Junior Bankers," *New York Times*, November 5, 2015. Retrieved from http://www.nytimes.com/2015/11/06/business/dealbook/goldman-sachs-rolls-out-new-policies-to-retain-junior-bankers.html?ribbon-ad-idx=3&rref=business/dealbook&module=Ribbon&version=context®ion=Header&action=click&contentCollection=DealBook&pgtype=article&_r=0

CHAPTER 4

1. Patricia Cohen, "One Company's New Minimum Wage: $70,000 a Year." *The New York Times*, April 13, 2015. Retrieved from http://www.nytimes.com/2015/04/14/business/owner-of-gravity-payments-a-credit-card-processor-is-setting-a-new-minimum-wage-70000-a-year.html?_r=0
2. "CEO Buys Short-Term Love - The Rush Limbaugh Show." Rush Limbaugh. N.p., April 15, 2015. Retrieved from http://www.rushlimbaugh.com/daily/2015/04/15/ceo_buys_short_term_love
3. Paul Davidson, "Does a $70,000 Minimum Wage Work?" *USA Today*, May 26, 2016. Gannett Satellite Information Network. Retrieved from http://www.usatoday.com/story/money/2016/05/26/does-70000-minimum-wage-work/84913242/
4. Jonathan Brill, "How Steve Jobs Got His Employees to Believe in Apple," *Time*, October 14, 2015. Retrieved from http://time.com/4068347/steve-jobs-apple-employee-strategy/
5. Interview of Carey Smith, conducted July 5, 2016, by Tim Vandehy.
6. Christian Jarrett and Joannah Ginsburg, *This Book Has Issues: Adventures in Popular Psychology*. (Crows Nest, N.S.W.: Allen & Unwin, 2008.)

CHAPTER 5

1. Molly Brown, "REI's Move to Close Black Friday Pays Off with 26 Percent Hike in Online Traffic," *GeekWire*. Retrieved from www.geekwire.com/2015/reis-move-to-close-black-friday-pays-off-in-more-online-traffic
2. Drew Harwell, "Starbucks' CEO Sent This Bizarre Memo Telling Baristas to Be Nicer Because of the Stock Turmoil," *Washington Post*, August 24, 2015. Retrieved from https://www.washingtonpost.com/news/business/wp/2015/08/24/starbucks-chief-sent-a-bizarre-memo-telling-baristas-to-be-nicer-because-of-the-stock-market/

3. Brigid Schulte, "A Company that Profits as It Pampers Workers," *The Washington Post*, October 25, 2014. Retrieved from https://www.washingtonpost.com/business/a-company-that-profits-as-it-pampers-workers/2014/10/22/d3321b34-4818-11e4-b72e-d60a9229cc10_story.htm
4. Megan McArdle, "Beware: Wal-Mart's Raises Are Not a Victory," *Bloomberg*, January 26, 2016. Retrieved from https://www.bloomberg.com/view/articles/2016-01-26/beware-wal-mart-s-raises-are-not-a-victory
5. Quentin Hardy, "Marc Benioff, Salesforce Chief, on the Strategic Benefits of Corporate Giving," *New York Times*, November 2, 2015. Retrieved from http://www.nytimes.com/2015/11/08/giving/marc-benioff-salesforce-chief-on-the-strategic-benefits-of-corporate-giving.html?_r=1
6. Jenny Che, "New Employees at Salesforce Volunteer Out of Office on First Day at Work," *The Huffington Post*, November 5, 2015. Retrieved from http://www.huffingtonpost.com/entry/salesforce-new-employees-volunteer-first-day_us_563a6c3de4b0307f2cabc7e5
7. M. Koenigs and D. Tranel, "Prefrontal Cortex Damage Abolishes Brand-Cued Changes in Cola Preference," *Social Cognitive and Affective Neuroscience* 3 (2008): 1–6. doi:10.1093/scan/nsm032
8. Meghan M. Biro, "Your Employer Brand Owns the Candidate Experience," *Forbes*, April 27, 2014. Retrieved from http://www.forbes.com/sites/meghanbiro/2014/04/27/your-employer-brand-owns-the-candidate-experience/#5b11120f5238

CHAPTER 6

1. ALDI careers website, "District Managers." Retrieved from www.careers.aldi.us/district.
2. Spencer Woodman, "Exclusive: Amazon Makes Even Temporary Warehouse Workers Sign 18-month Non-Competes," *The Verge*, March 26, 2015. Retrieved from www.theverge.com/2015/3/26/8280309/amazon-warehouse-jobs-exclusive-noncompete-contracts
3. Interview of David Behm, conducted September 27, 2016 by Tim Vandehy.
4. Ivan T. Robinson and Gary L. Cooper, *Personnel Psychology and Human Resources Management: A Reader for Students and Practitioners* (Hoboken, NJ: Wiley-Blackwell, 2010), 417.
5. Aaron Vehling, "At-Will Workers Can't Sue for Fraud, Texas High Court Says," *Law 360*, April 25, 2014. Retrieved from http://www.law360.com/articles/531843/at-will-workers-can-t-sue-for-fraud-texas-high-court-says
6. John Lilly, "Steve Jobs," *John's Tumblr*, October 9, 2011. Retrieved from http://lilly.tumblr.com/post/11230723028/steve-jobs
7. Michael Nesmith interview with Ken Plume, 2003. Retrived from http://asitecalledfred.com/2016/05/25/michael-nesmith-ken-plume-interview/

CHAPTER 7

1. Bureau of Economic Analysis, National Economic Accounts, "Table 1.1.5. Gross Domestic Product (A) (Q)," December 23, 2008. Retrieved from http://bea.gov/national/index.htm#gdp
2. "Uncompromising Commitment." Retrieved from http://www.uncompromisingcommitment.org/articles/2012/05/franklin-d-roosevelt/
3. Microfinance Barometer 2014/Convergences. Available at http://www.citigroup.com/citi/microfinance/data/lebarometre.pdf
4. Ibid.
5. Frederick Winslow Taylor, *The Principles of Scientific Management* (New York: Harper & Brothers, 1915).
6. Chris Argyris, *Understanding Organizational Behavior* (Homewood, IL: Dorsey Press, 1960).
7. D. M. Rousseau, (1989) "Psychological and Implied Contracts in Organizations," *Employee Responsibilities and Rights Journal* 2 (1989): 123.
8. Charlie O. Trevor and Anthony J. Nyberg, "Keeping Your Headcount When All About You Are Losing Theirs: Downsizing, Voluntary Turnover Rates, and the Moderating Role of HR Practices," *Academy of Management Journal* 51, no. 2 (April/May 2008): 259–276. doi:10.5465/AMJ.2008.31767250
9. Traron Moore, "The Impact of Psychological Contract Fulfillment on Employee Engagement in the Millennial Generation: The Moderating Effects of Generational Affiliation." Ph.D. dissertation, Georgia State University, 2014. Available at http://scholarworks.gsu.edu/cgi/viewcontent.cgi?article=1043&context=bus_admin_diss
10. L. Festinger, H. Riecken, and S. Schachter, *When Prophecy Fails* (Minneapolis, MN: University of Minnesota Press, 1956).
11. K. E. Weick, *Sensemaking in Organizations* (Thousand Oaks, CA: Sage Publications, 1995).
12. Interview of Scott Beck, conducted July 28, 2016 by Tim Vandehy.

CHAPTER 8

1. Carmen Tse, "Uber Driver Injured by Passenger in Attack Sues for Workers Comp," May 2, 2015. Retrieved from http://sfist.com/2015/05/02/uber_driver_workers_comp.php
2. Marissa Kendall, "Legal Threatdown: What's Chasing Uber?" December 22, 2015. Retrieved from http://www.law.com/sites/articles/2015/12/22/legal-threatdown-whats-chasing-uber/
3. Austin Carr, "The Secret to Airbnb's Freakishly Rapid Orgy Response: 'Scenario Planning,'" *Fast Company*, March 17, 2014. Available at https://www.fastcompany.com/3027798/the-secret-to-airbnbs-freakishly-rapid-orgy-response-scenario-planning

4. Lou Kerner, "A Look at the Data: Uber Is Losing Share to Lyft across the U.S. and Via in NYC," *Medium*, January 16, 2016. Retrieved from medium.com/@loukerner/a-look-at-the-data-uber-is-losing-share-to-lyft-across-the-u-s-and-via-in-nyc-703703f3fbc6#.kelju1xvq
5. V.S. Ramachandran and Sandra Blakeslee. *Phantoms in the Brain: Probing the Mysteries of the Human Mind.* (New York: William Morrow, 1998.)
6. Marjan Houshmand, "Escaping Bullying: The Simultaneous Impact of Individual and Unit-Level Bullying on Turnover Intentions," *Human Relations* 65, no. 7 (July 2012): 901–918. doi: 10.1177/0018726712445100
7. Our thanks to Kristin Chapman, who helped us understand the concept and importance of Chronos and Kairos moments.
8. Maren Hogan, "How to Get Employee Onboarding Right," *Forbes,* May 29, 2015. Retrieved from http://www.forbes.com/sites/theyec/2015/05/29/how-to-get-employee-onboarding-right
9. John Kammeyer-Mueller, Connie Wanberg, Alex Rubenstein, and Zhaoli Song, "Support, Undermining, and Newcomer Socialization: Fitting In during the First 90 Days," *Academy of Management Journal* 56, no. 4 (August 2013): 1104–1124.
10. Stan Silverman, "VW Employees Responsible for 'Dieselgate': Where's the Legal, Moral, & Ethical Compass?" *Philadelphia Business Journal*, October 5, 2015.
11. William Boston, "Volkswagen Suspends More Employees," *Wall Street Journal*, October 26, 2015.
12. Elizabeth Whitman, "Volkswagen Scandal Update 2016: Former Employee Sues, Seeking Whistleblower Protections over Data Deletion," *International Business Times*, March 13, 2016.
13. Christoph Rauwald, "VW Said to Cut 30,000 Jobs, Save $3.9 Billion in Labor Pact." Bloomberg.com. Bloomberg, Nov. 18, 2016. Retrieved from https://www.bloomberg.com/news/articles/2016-11-18/vw-said-to-cut-23-000-jobs-save-3-9-billion-with-labor-pact
14. "Media Report: VW Execs Will Not Forego [*sic*] Bonuses." Retrieved from www.dw.com/en/media-report-vw-execs-will-not-forego-bonuses/a-19172295, accessed April 19, 2016.
15. Maurice E. Schweitzer, Alison Wood Brooks, and Adam D. Galinsky, "The Organizational Apology," *Harvard Business Review* (September 2015, pp. 44-52.)
16. Jessica Durando, "BP's Tony Hayward: 'I'd Like My Life Back,'" *USA Today*, June 1, 2010. Retrieved from http://content.usatoday.com/communities/greenhouse/post/2010/06/bp-tony-hayward-apology/1#.V5kb72WfTEI

CHAPTER 9

1. From "Principles of Research," a speech delivered at Max Planck's 60th birthday celebration, 1918; published in *Mein Weltbild*, by Albert Einstein (Amsterdam: Querido Verlag, 1934); reprinted in *Ideas and Opinions*, by Albert Einstein (New York: Crown, 1954), pp. 224-227; *Expanded*, p. 235

2. Interview of Scott Beck, conducted July 28, 2016 by Tim Vandehy.
3. Interview of Scott Beck, conducted July 28, 2016 by Tim Vandehy.
4. Interview of Kevin Ricklefs, conducted July 26, 2016 by Tim Vandehy.
5. Interview of Mark Law, conducted July 25, 2016 by Tim Vandehy.
6. Barb, "Case Study of Culture Change at Life's WORC," Leaders In Motion, January 11, 2013. Retrieved from www.leadersinmotion.net/case-study-of-culture-change-at-lifes-worc/

Index